D1460679

ALCOHOL, DRINKING, DRUNKENNESS

Alcohol, Drinking, Drunkenness
(Dis)Orderly Spaces

MARK JAYNE
University of Manchester, UK

GILL VALENTINE
University of Leeds, UK

SARAH L. HOLLOWAY
Loughborough University, UK

ASHGATE

Published by
Ashgate Publishing Limited
Wey Court East
Union Road
Farnham
Surrey, GU9 7PT
England

Ashgate Publishing Company
Suite 420
101 Cherry Street
Burlington
VT 05401-4405
USA

www.ashgate.com

British Library Cataloguing in Publication Data
Jayne, Mark, 1970–
  (Dis)orderly geographies : alcohol, drinking, drunkenness.
  1. Drinking of alcoholic beverages. 2. Alcoholism. 3. Human geography.
  I. Title II. Valentine, Gill, 1965– III. Holloway, Sarah L., 1970–
  394.1'3'09–dc22

Library of Congress Cataloging-in-Publication Data
Jayne, Mark, 1970–
  Alcohol, drinking, drunkeness : (dis)orderly spaces / by Mark Jayne, Gill Valentine and Sarah L. Holloway.
      p. cm.
  Includes bibliographical references and index.
  ISBN 978-0-7546-7160-2 (hardback : alk. paper) 1. Drinking of alcoholic beverages—Case studies. 2. Drunkenness (Criminal law)—Case studies. I. Valentine, Gill, 1965– II. Holloway, Sarah L., 1970– III. Title.
  HV5035.J38 2011
  362.2920941—dc22

2010034762

ISBN 9780754671602 (hbk)
ISBN 9781409423300 (ebk)

Mixed Sources
Product group from well-managed forests and other controlled sources
www.fsc.org Cert no. SA-COC-1565
© 1996 Forest Stewardship Council
FSC

Printed and bound in Great Britain by
MPG Books Group, UK

Contents

List of Tables

Acknowledgements

We would like to thank the Joseph Rowntree Foundation for supporting the research presented in this book. In particular, we are very grateful to Charlie Lloyd for his encouragement and advice throughout the project. We are also grateful to the advisory group for their valuable contributions to the development of the research: Mike Atkinson (formerly, Eden Valley Primary Care Trust), Jennie Hammond (Stoke-on-Trent Drug and Alcohol Action), Anne Jenkins (Alcohol Concern), Andrew McNeill (Institute of Alcohol Studies), Mandy Nevin (Alcohol and Drug Services in Staffordshire), David Poley (The Portman Group), Gregor Russell (formely Director of Commissioning, Stoke-on-Trent Primary Care Trust), David Sibley (University of Leeds), Betsy Thom (Middlesex University) and Rebecca Wagstaff (Cumbria Primary Care Trust). We also wish to acknowledge the contribution of Mahmood Mizra and Tassnim Hussain who conducted the interviews with members of the Pakistani Muslim community in Stoke-on-Trent and Paul Norman (University of Leeds), who advised on the analysis of some of the quantitative data. Charlotte Knell worked as a research assistant on the project, undertaking fieldwork in Eden, and we want to thank her for her hard work and commitment to the project.

Mark would like to thank his colleagues at the University of Manchester and 'down the road' at Manchester Metropolitan University, as well as David Bell, Mike Leyshon, Slavomira Ferencuhova, the Wollongong Boys, Phil Hubbard, Dr and Mrs Potts, Dr Jon Hill, Mark Adams and in particular 'Evans the Steam'. Special thanks to Daisy.

Professor Sarah Holloway is a Philip Leverhulme Prize winner and gratefully acknowledges The Leverhulme Trust's support for her research.

The Authors would like to thank Carolyn Court, Val Rose and Sarah Horsley at Ashgate for their patience and support.

Chapters in this book draw, in parts, on empirical material and arguments published elsewhere. The authors and publishers would like to thank copyright holders for permission to reproduce the following material:

Sage Publications Ltd, London, Los Angeles, New Delhi, Singapore and Washington DC for permission to reproduce from: Jayne, M., Valentine, G., and Holloway S.L. (2008), 'Geographies of Alcohol, Drinking and Drunkenness: A Review of Progress', *Progress in Human Geography* 32/2: 247–263; Jayne, M., Holloway, S.L. and Valentine, G. (2006), 'Drunk and Disorderly: Alcohol, Urban Life and Public Space', *Progress in Human Geography* 30/4: 451–468.

Routledge, London and New York for permission to reproduce from: Jayne, M., Valentine, G. and Holloway, S.L. (2008), 'Fluid Boundaries – "British" Binge Drinking and "European" Civility: Alcohol and the Production and Consumption of Public Space', *Space and Polity* 12/1: 81–100; Jayne, M., Valentine, G., and Holloway S.L. (2008), 'The Place of Drink: Geographical Contributions to Alcohol Studies', *Drugs: Education, Prevention and Policy*: 1–14.

Pion Limited, London for permssion to reproduce from: Valentine, G., Holloway, S.L., Jayne, M. (2010), 'Contemporary Cultures of Abstinence and the Night-time Economy: Muslim Attitudes Towards Alcohol and the Implications for Social Cohesion', *Environment and Planning A* 42/1: 8–22.

Elsevier, London, for permission to reproduce from: Valentine, G., Holloway, S.L., Jayne, M. (2010), 'Generational Patterns of Alcohol Consumption: Continuity and Change', *Health and Place* 16/5: 916–925; Holloway, S.L., Valentine, G. and Jayne, M. (2009), Masculinities, Femininities and the Geographies of Public and Private Drinking Landscapes,' *Geoforum* 40/5: 821–831; Valentine, G., Holloway, S. L., Knell, C., and Jayne, M. (2008), 'Drinking Places: Young People and Cultures of Alcohol Consumption in Rural Environments', *Journal of Rural Studies* 24: 28–40.

John Wiley and Sons, London, for permission to reproduce from: Holloway, S.L., Jayne, M. and Valentine, G. (2008), 'Sainsbury's is my Local': English Alcohol Policy, Domestic Drinking Practices and the Meaning of Home,' *Transaction of the Institute of British Geographers* 33: 532–547; Jayne, M., Valentine, G. and Holloway, S.L. (2010), 'Emotional, Embodied and Affective Geographies of Alcohol, Drinking and Drunkenness', *Transactions of the Institute of British Geographers* 35/4: 540–554.

Introduction
Geographies of Alcohol, Drinking and Drunkenness

This is the first book with a focus on geographies of alcohol, drinking and drunkenness. While disciplines such as anthropology, sociology, criminology, politics, social policy, and the health and medical sciences have a long tradition of exploring the role of alcohol, drinking and drunkenness in peoples' lives, geographers have only recently began engage in this area of research. In the context of the voluminous number of books, journal articles, book chapters and official reports, research undertaken by geographers has yet to make a significant impact on debates. Nonetheless, recent work has shown that geographers have much to offer academic, policy and popular understandings of the complex political, economic, social, cultural and spatial practices and processes bound up with alcohol, drinking and drunkenness. The aim of this book is to build on that progress. By presenting theoretically informed empirical research undertaken in the UK and drawing on writing from around the world, we argue that space and place must be conceptualized as key constituents of practices and processes relating to alcohol, drinking and drunkenness. In doing so, we foreground the ways in which geographical approaches to studying alcohol, drinking and drunkenness can contribute to debates within and beyond the discipline.

While geographers are relative newcomers, a geographical focus has nonetheless, been a traditional feature of alcohol research agendas. Consideration of spatial relations, practices and concepts focused on issues such as distinctions between public and private, the city and the countryside, boundaries and transgressions, visibility and invisibility, centrality and marginality, national and local identities (and so on) have been a key feature of alcohol research. Indeed, theorists have addressed a diverse range of topics relating to legislation, policy and policing; production, marketing and retail; consumption, identity, lifestyle and forms of sociability at a variety of different transnational, national, regional and local spatial scales. However, despite alcohol studies including significant geographical research, there has been little consideration of the ways in which space and place are active constituents of the topics being studied. In these terms the geographical focus of alcohol research has tended to simply offer a location or focus, rather than as a key theoretical or empirical element of the research at hand.

Moreover, despite the large amount of work across the social and medical sciences alcohol, drinking and drunkenness has tended to be considered in contradictory ways, with little dialogue existing between disciplines. For example, in the social sciences there is a clear distinction between, on one hand, consideration of lawlessness, violence and fear of crime, and in response, zero tolerance policing, changing legislation and policy and a competing body of work with the theoretical goal of moving beyond the limiting pathologizing of alcohol consumption in order to investigate the everyday social relations and cultural practices bound up with drinking. Despite voluminous findings and valuable debate, there have been de facto and/or fragmented research agendas with little sustained inter- (or trans) disciplinary dialogue. Research that has sought to develop new theoretical frameworks, to draw together political and economic with social and cultural (or even spatial) issues has failed to have any significant impact on the direction of alcohol studies research.

In this book we address this impasse and in doing so we highlight how studying geographies of alcohol, drinking and drunkenness can contribute to academic, political, policy and popular debates. This introductory chapter begins with a review of writing by geographers and theorists beyond the discipline. This is followed by a brief introduction to the ways in which each chapter seeks to advance understanding of the geographies of alcohol, drinking and drunkenness by developing sophisticated and nuanced understanding of the role that space and place play in people's drinking practices. Throughout we foreground arguments and empirical material that make connections between different people, places, practices and processes, addressing similarities, differences and mobilities at different spatial scales. Each chapter explicitly shows the ways in which human geography is developing important new insights that add value to our understanding of alcohol, drinking and drunkenness.

Alcohol Research and Geographical Approaches

A review of alcohol studies literature uncovers work that addresses the ways in which alcohol, drinking and drunkenness are differentially and discursively constructed in specific spaces and places. A large amount of research has for example investigated spatial patterns of drinking and drink related issues. This includes, quantitative research looking at the relationship between outlet density and drink related problems in the US (Tatlow et al. 2000), patterns and variations in alcohol content and spirit measures in Scotland (Gill and Donaghy 2004) and analysis of consumption habits and consumers use of drinking venues (Treno et al. 2000). There is also a significant body of writing concerning national, regional or local alcohol related legislation, initiatives and policies, as well as work that draws on large scale transnational statistical reports and cross-cultural surveys. For example, studies include, an investigation of alcohol control and policy in Finland (Alavaikko and Osterberg 2000), research into the relationship between drinking and gender in nine European Countries (Allaman et al. 2000), a study of students' drinking in eighteen countries (Smart and Ogbourne 2000), a survey of the Russian population's drinking habits (Bobak et al. 1999), and various local initiates in Europe (Comedia 1991; Ramsey 1990), the US (Wittman 1997), and

Australia (Lindsay 2005). There are also a growing number of large transnati
surveys and projects (WHO 2000, 2001, 2004; ESPAD 2004; ECAS 2002).

Theorists have also investigated the relationship between place, drinking
patterns and identity, lifestyle and forms of sociability in a large number of
different locations around the world. Studies have focused on drinking in
Andalusia, drinking amongst female entertainers in Egypt, an analysis of the
relationship between drinking wine and masculinity in France, beer drinking in
Hungary, commensality and drinking in Greek agriculture, drinking and fishing
in Ireland, Norwegian domestic drinking parties, football and drinking in Malta,
tribal drinking in Northern Cameroon, drinking in Mexico, and a study of the
relationship between drinking and slavery in the British Caribbean (see for
example, Allaman et al. 2000; Bobak et al. 1999; de Garine and de Garine 2001;
Gefou-Madianou 1992; Holt 2006; Share 2003; Wilson 2005). Other work has
considered drinking and gender in India (Chatterjee 2003), gender and sexuality in
San Fransisco (Bloomfield 1993), drinking and young people in Vietnam (Thomas
2002), young people in rural areas of Australia and Wales (Jones 2002; Kelly and
Kowalyszyn 2003; Kraack and Kenway 2002), underage drinking in Barcelona
(Vives 2000), masculinity and identity in Newcastle-upon-Tyne (Nayak 2003),
alcohol related service provision for Indian, Chinese and Pakistani young people
in Glasgow (Heim et al. 2004), Sikh, Hindu, Muslim and white male drinking in
the West Midlands (Cochrane and Bal 1990), African-Caribbean and South Asians
drinking patterns in the UK (McKeigue and Karmi 1993), and research that asked
respondents whether they think that it is acceptable for Australian supermodel Elle
McPherson to drink beer (Pettigrew 2002).

Such research has importantly generated rich and detailed findings in order to
show how specific issues related to alcohol, drinking and drunkenness unfold in
particular spaces and places. While these studies offer important findings, there
has nonetheless been a failure to formulate research agendas that also offer the
opportunity to pursue a more integrated understanding of how interpenetration
of political, economic, social, cultural and spatial elements impact upon alcohol,
drinking and drunkenness at particular spatial scales in either theoretical and
empirical terms. For example, while work relevantly identifies issues that are of
geographical importance, there has been a tendency to gloss over the extent to
which space and place are key constituents of the issues at hand. While each of the
above examples focuses on national or local levels, often pursuing comparisons
between different spaces and places, research has generally tended to shy away
from making connections, describing similarities, differences, or mobilities
between case studies. This has ensured a lack of theoretical arguments that translate
beyond specific people and spaces and places, other than dialectical approaches
which consider alcohol as either a social/medical problem or as a social or cultural
practice. While there has been some attempts to conjoin these issues via a focus on
transnational, national and local levels (for example, Holder 2000; Harrison 1998;
Jones 1987) there has been little success in developing perspective that translate
beyond the empirical evidence generated at particular spatial scales.

A useful way to elaborate this point is to consider debates around 'European' drinking patterns'. At a Europe-wide scale researchers in the field of public health have started to question the relevance of the traditional dichotomy between 'wet' Mediterranean countries (where wine is the customary drink, alcohol consumption is high but unlikely to result in intoxication) and 'dry' Northern European countries such as the UK (where beer or spirits are the established drink, alcohol consumption is lower overall but more likely to result in intoxication, and access to alcohol has been more closely regulated) (ECAS 2002; Knibbe et al. 1996). Researchers have questioned whether there has been a homogenization in both drinking rates (as consumption has increased in the 'dry' countries and fallen in the 'wet' countries) and beverage choice (with wine consumption up in 'dry' countries and down markedly in 'wet' countries, beer has become more popular in non-traditional markets, and a growth in new beverages such as alcopops across the board) (Allamani et al. 2000; Leifman, 2001). However, while there has been a questioning of the limits to this apparently clear cut picture of homogenization in European regulatory regimes and drinking practices, there has not been a systematic attempt to undertake research to explore this issue.

For example, studies of European drinking policy and consumption practices have been undertaken in three ways. Firstly, public health researchers (often funded by supra-national bodies such as the WHO and the EU) have employed large-scale, cross-national quantitative studies which have made useful but broad-brush comparisons between European countries, often focusing on high consumption amongst particular social groups such as women or young people (ECAS, 2002: ESPAD 2003; WHO 2000, 2001, 2004). Secondly, a similar focus on alcohol consumption-related medical problems has been seen in quantitative studies working at a sub-national scale (Gmel et al. 2000; Knibbe et al. 2001; Plant et al. 2000). Thirdly, researchers in a diversity of disciplines (including medical sciences, psychology, sociology and human geography) have undertaken smaller scale qualitative research which tends to investigate consumption of alcohol as a medical/social problem for specific social groups (Beccaria and Sande 2003).

Moreover, even when research offers a useful antidote to general approaches, a number of weaknesses can be identified. For example, focusing on specific places and people via study of consumption, identity, lifestyle and forms of sociability, research has focused on gender differences and drinking patterns (Ettorre 2000; Plant 1997; Waterson 2000; Harnett et al. 2000), gender and sexuality (Bloomfield 1993), masculinity, femininity and ethnicity (Shaikh and Nax 2000), women who drink and expose themselves (Hugh-Jones et al. 2005), women who drink and fight (Day et al. 2003), men and violence (Benson and Archer 2002) and drinking amongst various black and minority ethnic groups, and so on (Share 2003; Stivers 2000). Despite considering topics at different spatial scales, space and place are mainly addressed as passive backdrops to the issues being considered. Location, context and the relationships between the people and places tends to be considered as a peripheral issue. Such limitations are perhaps best evidenced by the lack of attempt to join up, to compare or contrast research in different contexts and at different spatial scales. Thus, while such research is a corrective to more general approaches the connections, similarities, differences and mobilities between drinking practices and contexts at either general or specific levels are not considered in a clear way.

There are, of course, a number of exceptions where writers are indeed attempting such a project. Writers have usefully identified, for instance, the conflicts and trade offs between legal and 'common-sense' definitions of drunkenness and policing policy (including sensitivity towards differences in local cultural practices, behaviour, speech and so on), unpacking how discourses of pleasure are bound up and accounted for in the legislative and policy making process (Levi and Valverde 2001; O'Malley and Valverde 2004; Valverde 2003). Other useful examples, include research into the characterization of the 'larger lout' by the Thatcherite government, young male drinkers in the North East of England and street drinking in Vietnam (see Hunt and Slatterlee 1981, 1986, 1991; Gofton 1990; Nayak 2003; Thomas 2002). Such work contextualizes how local, regional and national assertions of resistant identity are differentially constructed in terms of broader processes – thus considering alcohol, drinking and drunkenness in terms of political and economic change and conflict via social and cultural relations at various spatial scales. This writing is particularly useful in allowing comparisons of the ways in which legislative, policing, policy and health issues are mobilized around specific issues and specific groups of people, in different spaces and places. Despite such exceptions studies that seek to draw together conflicting and seemingly entrenched epistemological and ontological positions within alcohol studies remain small in number and are relatively marginalized.

In summary, we suggest that there are two important issues which arise from reviewing geographical contributions to alcohol studies research. Firstly, there has been an under-theorization of the role and impact that space and place have on the differential and discursive construction of issues relating to alcohol, drinking and drunkenness. In these terms human geography has much to offer theoretical and empirical debates concerning the importance of both historical and contemporary spatial practices and processes relating to alcohol, drinking and drunkenness and their unique position in wider constellations of political, economic, social, cultural and spatial relations (Massey 1995; Castree 2003). Secondly, and underpinning the theoretical and substantive points argued in this section, it is our view that engaging with the different ways that alcohol, drinking and drunkenness are considered and approached by different theorists and disciplines must be a central concern for human geographers. Research into alcohol, drinking and drunkenness is undertaken in diverse and significantly different ways, often with little dialogue between, or reference to different theoretical or methodological traditions. For example, drink related issues are studied as a central or peripheral topic, considered as a causal or contributory factor. Alcohol is at once a social problem, a leisure activity, a pleasure, an accelerator of violence, central to identity formation and so on. While these are all, of course, relevant areas of study, there has been little sustained attempt to engage in theoretical and empirical debate concerning the different ways in which alcohol studies research frames and addresses the practices and processes (and people and places) being studied.

Geography and Alcohol, Drinking and Drunkenness

Over the past decade, geographers have looked at alcohol, drinking and drunkenness in terms of a number of different topics, with varying focus and depth of interest. These include for example studies of the entertainment/night time economy (Chatterton and Hollands 2002, 2003; Hubbard 2005; Latham 2003; Latham and McCormack 2004; Malbon 1999; Thomas and Bromley 2000), geographies of food (Bell 2005; Bell and Binnie 2006; Bell and Valentine 1997); pub life and identity (Edensor 2006; Hall 1992; Kneale 1999, 2004; Leyshon 2005, Maye et al. 2005; Valentine 2007a); temperance (Kneale 2001); family life (Lowe et al. 1993); the relationship between drinking and health (Philo et al. 2002; Twigg and Jones 2000); historical geographies of wine production and consumption (Unwin 1991), the distribution of working men's clubs (Purvis 1998); and policing and urban public space (Bromley et al. 2000, 2002, 2003; Jayne et al. 2006; Raco 2003).

Such geographical work offers vital insights into the ways in which space and place are key constituents of a diverse set of issues relating to alcohol, drinking and drunkenness. It is clear then, over a relatively short period of time that there has been a bourgeoning interest in alcohol drinking and drunkenness amongst geographers. To a certain degree however, geography has mirrored alcohol studies research by focusing on specific issues in specific places that while generating rich and diverse findings has been based on a de facto and fragmented research agenda. Nonetheless, writing by geographers *is* adding value to knowledge and debates within geography as well as more broadly to alcohol studies research by pursuing theoretical and empirically nuanced work aimed at tying together geographies of political, economic, social, cultural and spatial practices and processes.

For example, in *Urban Nightscapes: Youth Cultures, Pleasure, Spaces and Corporate Power* (2003), Chatterton and Hollands undertake ethnographic research that is grounded in theories of wider processes of capital accumulation and restructuring and look at the interpenetration between processes of production, regulation, consumption, identity and representation. In simple terms, they look at who and what is involved in producing nightlife spaces (for example, designing, marketing, selling, property markets, corporate strategies etc.); who and what is involved in regulating them (for example, laws and legislation, surveillance, entrance points, codes of conduct); and who and what is involved in consuming them (for example, lived experience, perceptions and stereotypes). Thus, while they have a specific focus on young people and urban nightlife and not drinking *per se*, their work is very useful here in identifying how geographers can offer a conceptually and empirically 'joined-up' approach.

Other geographers have begun to move beyond such generalized depictions to show that far than being homogenized, drinking is a varied activity constructed through diverse practices and experiences. Scratching the surface appearance of urban transformations identifies not a homogenized, purified set of spaces and experiences but something more complicated and contested. Studies have sought to connect the general and specific ways in which broad political, economic, social, cultural and spatial practices and processes relating to alcohol, drinking and drunkenness play out in different ways, at different times and for different people in different spaces and places. For example, Alan Latham (2003, 173), while recognizing the pervasiveness of social divisions that have characterized the city over the past thirty years, highlights that general depictions of urban life lack understanding of day-to-day uses of space, which suggests an idealization of the city against which 'real' cities do not match.

Latham's (2003, 1709) ethnographic study of two streets in Auckland, New Zealand uncovers a public culture that is underpinned by tolerance, diversity and creative energy, with a mixing of post-industrial lifestyles, with sexually polymorphous and industrial male public cultures co-inhabiting in hotels and pubs. Latham suggests that there is a mix of 'self-consciously worldly spaces' and traditional pubs, where 'groups are mixed sex and not infrequently of openly mixed sexualities, and if people get drunk that is rarely the main purpose of the evening but rather a rather pleasant side effect of the night's socializing' (2003, 1712). He identifies a mixing of vernacular and gentrified drinkscapes, and a convivial ecology, which can be seen to spill into the streets, generating 'new solidarities and new collectivities' and a greater sense of belonging (Latham 2003, 1719). Edensor (2006) makes a similar point about the Keg and Marlin pub located on the re-developed waterfront of Port Louis, Mauritius. The Keg and Marlin allows the ethnic and religious divisions that characterizes the city/island to be (temporarily at least) challenged. This drinking space allows social mixing and suspension of tension and struggle via drinking and drunken forms of sociability.

Similarly, other researchers has focused on the interpenetration of a number of issues relating to legislation, production, consumption, service provision and health issues through consideration of class, gender, ethnicity, sexuality, age, urbanity/rurality, public/private (and so on) via engagement with research into social geographies. Valentine et al. (2007a, 2007b) discus how, when, why and for whom drinking alcohol is discursively constructed as a 'problem', one that demands both government intervention and the development and enactment of specific tailored policing strategies in the UK. By focusing on complex and spatialized ways in which drinking amongst young people is framed as a 'problem' – differently in urban and rural areas – research has shown the importance of a more sustained consideration of the ways in which alcohol, drinking and drunkenness is problematized – and when it is not (Jayne et al. 2006; Valentine et al. 2007a).

Such work exemplifies that in seeking to unpack the connections, similarities, differences and motilities relating to alcohol related issues at different spatial scales geographers are achieving degrees of success that is rare in alcohol studies writing. Nonetheless, although engaging in study of alcohol, drinking and drunkenness geographers have failed to address fundamental questions about how the topics, issues, approaches and theoretical terrain that they are studying is approached more broadly. While to a certain degree this criticism is unfair given that such a project has not been a stated concern of geographers' engagement with alcohol, drinking and drunkenness, we argue that such a goal is important if fledgling geographies are not to replicate some of the weaknesses and impasses of alcohol studies research.

Katz's (2001) concept of counter-topographies is particularly useful here in showing the ways in which geographers can address weaknesses in alcohol studies research. Katz use of the geographical term *topography*, referring both to the detailed description of a particular location and the features that comprise the landscape itself – physical geographers use contour lines to connect places at a uniform altitude to reveal the three-dimensional form of the terrain. Katz (2001) adaptation of these terms can be applied to drinking related issues by using counter-topographies in a number ways. This approach is useful to describe the interpenetration of political, economic, social, cultural and spatial 'features' relating to drinking landscapes within and between specific spaces and places. Importantly, this approach represents a conceptual technique in which theoretical contour lines can be used to connect spaces and places analytically. In doing so, it is possible to trace general relations, practices and processes and to identify their common (and unique) unfolding on the ground. Indeed, this conceptual approach is also useful in imagining different kinds of practical responses and the effectiveness of resultant actions. In this way, geographers spatial knowledges can be used to transcend the specificities of the localities in which they were gathered and can be mobilized in ways that offer possibilities for making wider theoretical, political and policy connections.

This approach has much to offer alcohol studies. Such work provides a conceptual framework to engage with debates concerning the ways in which alcohol related issues are a key part of political, economic and cultural life, supported and nurtured not only at the level of vernacular but through political and planning discourses. However, concern can also be expressed about the ways in which alcohol, drinking and drunkenness are being mobilized to pursue such agendas. On one hand, the proliferation of diverse research into alcohol, drinking and drunkenness by geographers can be argued to offer a relevant way of addressing underlying assumptions and conceptualizations of the relationship between space and place and alcohol, drinking and drunkenness in critical and creative ways. Nonetheless, it is also possible to argue that in pursuing such an approach geographers are currently utilizing alcohol, drinking and drunkenness as an empirical set of practices and processes that are simply being used to investigate already existing and newly emerging conceptual, methodological and policy agendas within the discipline.

While these approaches are undoubtedly relevant we argue that it is vital for geographers to begin to question the theoretical and methodological approaches that are being mobilized in order to consider alcohol, drinking and drunkenness in a more detailed and sustained way. Adding alcohol, drinking and drunkenness to the cannon of human geography research is, of course, an important theoretical and methodological goal. Nonetheless, in doing so human geographers must engage more fully with the strengths and weaknesses of the alcohol research that geographers' are drawingon in order to frame and underpin their own work. We argue that it is through this challenging agenda that human geography will add value to the advances already made and lead to research that has highly significant conceptually and empirically contributions to make to alcohol studies agendas.

Examples throughout this chapter have shown that epistemologies of generality or specificity (or both combined) have given geographers the opportunity to contribute to both disciplinary and wider debates (see Castree 2005; Massey 1995). However, by making connections, unpacking similarities, differences and mobilities between supranational, national, regional, and local spatial scales, geographers are also producing work that is conceptually and empirically groundbreaking. In these terms human geographers are currently investigating complex interpenetrations of political, economic, social, cultural and spatial issues to a degree not achieved in any coherent or sustained way by alcohol studies research.

However, this chapter also strikes a note of caution. While geographers have focused on developing new areas of research – producing ground breaking interventions for human geography into this area of research – there has been a failure to engage in a detailed and clear way with epistemological, ontological and methodological genealogies of broader alcohol studies research. Pursuing such an agenda is of course, by no means an easy task – tackling orthodoxies and assumptions that conjoin and separate research both within and across disciplinary boundaries offers a significant challenge. Indeed, we do not claim to present any clever approaches to the problem of fragmentation or solutions to the competing approaches that characterize alcohol studies research. However, what is clear is that there is a need for geographers to engage in establishing the 'translation-rules' for dialogue between human geography and broader research into alcohol, drinking and drunkenness (Castree 2005, 544). Geographers need to address the different ways that alcohol related issues are considered, measured, conceived and theorized, and moreover to engage with the theoretical and empirical frameworks and impasses that exist in alcohol studies research. To this end, this book seeks to highlight the important role that geographical research into alcohol, drinking and drunkenness can play in advancing both disciplinary and broader alcohol studies research agendas.

Reading (Dis)Orderly Spaces

A key feature of this book is that the chapters include quantitative and qualitative findings from a research project undertaken in the UK (see Appendix 1). Interviews were recorded and transcribed, and along with the participant observation material were analyzed using conventional qualitative techniques. The quotes presented throughout the book are anonymized and verbatim; editing is highlighted. By combining our research findings with studies and writing focusing on different spaces and places throughout the world we seek to avoid abstraction or over-simplification, but instead to develop understanding of the complexity and nuances of drinking and drunkenness without shying away from identifying broader trends.

Chapter 1 focuses on alcohol, drinking and drunkenness in urban areas. We consider the ways in which the 'evils of drink' and alcohol related violence and disorder have been a central feature of political and policy concern, popular debate and everyday life from the late eighteenth century right up to the present day. We review writing that has sought to describe how drinking practices and associated legislative, policy and policing strategies are associated with structural urban change and highlight how alcohol has been conceptualized as either a social or medial problem or viewed as a vital part of the social and cultural practices of city life. We argue that there has been an overly dualistic approach to understanding alcohol and drunkenness in the city, and highlight the need for research that looks at the complexity and diversity of urban alcohol consumption.

Chapter 2 moves from The City to consider drinking in The Countryside. We review writing focused on the ways in which attitudes towards alcohol, drinking and drunkenness are bound up with ideological notions of 'the rural idyll' and connections between humans and nature. Presenting evidence from different rural areas from around the world, the chapter highlights how alcohol consumption is bound up with particular issues associated with class, gender, isolation and so on. The chapter then focuses on how concerns surrounding young people drinking in the UK can be read alongside both rural restructuring and concerns over 'moral panics' associated with urban drinking are being transferred to, and translated in the countryside

Chapter 3 considers drinking at home and reviews academic and policy literature in order to explore why the domestic realm is often ignored. In doing so, we build on the argument made in the previous chapter that public and private drinking environments are inextricably linked, and explore what alcohol means to people as they move into and out of their homes. The chapter looks at who drinks at home, why, and with whom. We conclude by emphasizing how ideologies of the home underpin domestic drinking practices. We unpack the profound influences that mediate our understanding of domestic life and how these serve to insulate those drinking to harmful or hazardous levels in their homes from concern.

Chapter 4 focuses on gender in order to consider how drinking practices and behaviours are differentially and discursively constructed in different ways for men and women. We highlight how drinking is shaped through a gendered lens of ideas about appropriate masculinities and femininities. Our purpose in this chapter is to interrogate this apparently well accepted fact in order to uncover the ways these practices emerge and the form they take. We offer a snapshot of contemporary drinking practices in our study areas, in order to highlight not only their gendered nature, but crucially intra-gender differences between different groups of men, as well as different groups of women. We investigate the importance of gendered moralities in shaping drinking practices in public and private locations, and at the same time uncover the significance of other forms of social difference in diverse drinking cultures.

Chapter 5 attends to concerns that beyond North America the relationship between ethnicity and alcohol, drinking and drunkenness has been relatively ignored. In doing so, we seek to understand the role of alcohol in the lives' of Pakistani Muslims in our urban case study area. We theorize alcohol as an 'absent present' in a culture of abstention in order to understand the conflicts and tensions bound up with significant levels of alcohol consumption and how this effects access to and use public space. We show the complex and sophisticated ways in which Pakistani Muslims negotiate and make sense of their own, and others drinking, and non-drinking, in order to add new perspectives to debates about social cohesion in the contemporary urban nigh-time economy. The chapter also reflects on the consequences of a culture of abstinence for alcohol support services.

Chapter 6 builds on long-standing concern with life course and families in alcohol research by focusing on the oft-ignored issue of generational changes in attitudes too, and practices of alcohol consumption. We highlight continuities and discontinuities in drinking practices across the generations and consider how family structure and changing parenting styles are impacting on how attitudes and practices around alcohol are communicates in family contexts between different generations. We also discuss how patterns of continuity and change have a number of important policy implications.

Chapter 7 turns attention to the emotional and embodied geographies bound up with alcohol, drinking and drunkenness. We show that while emotions and bodies have been focused on in a significant amount of writing about alcohol, drinking and drunkenness the topic has tended to be approached in an implicit manner. We discuss, 'memories', 'rites of passage' and 'emotional talk' in order to make connections between the complex interpenetration of biological, psychological, physiological and political, economic, social, cultural and spatial practices and processes bound up with alcohol, drinking and drunkenness. We argue that geographers are developing fruitful and productive research agendas that offer much to broader alcohol research.

In the Afterword 'One for the Road' we raise a glass to toast the progress made by geographers who study alcohol, drinking and drunkenness. We outline and summarize the key themes covered in the book, re-visit important debates and case studies, draw links across the chapters and highlight future research agendas. In particular, we challenge geographers to pursue theoretical and empirical advances which make significant contributions to the study of alcohol, drinking and drunkenness within and beyond the discipline as well as making important interventions in political, policy and popular debates.

Chapter 1
The City

From the late eighteenth century to the present day alcohol, drinking and drunkenness have been a central feature of political and policy concern, popular debate and everyday life in urban areas. Fears over the 'evil of drink' and attempts to regulate and police alcohol consumption and drunken behaviour that were central to the bourgeois modernist project and vision of urban life during the eighteenth and nineteenth centuries are shown to be mirrored in contemporary depictions of urban areas blighted by alcohol related violence and disorder. A significant amount or research has sought to describe how people's drinking practices and associated legislative, policy and policing strategies are associated with structural urban change. While this research has produced valuable understanding of how alcohol, drinking and drunkenness is bound up with political, economic, social and spatial changes in our cities, studies have overwhelmingly focused on alcohol as a social or medial problem. In contrast other theorists have sought to show how alcohol, drinking and drunkenness are social and cultural practices bound up with sociability, conviviality, the mixing of social groups and engagements with strangers. This chapter considers these competing conceptualizations.

The 'Evils of Drink' and the Modern City

In offering the following quote from the young Frederick Engels in the 1840s Warren Schivelbusch (1992, 147–148) reflects on how commentators of the time observed that despite the emergence of modern industrial life, excess drinking associated with the uncivilized sixteenth century continued to dominate people's lives:

> It is not surprising that the workers should drink heavily. Sheriff Alison asserts that 30,000 workers are drunk in Glasgow every Saturday night. And this is certainly no underestimate … It is particularly on Saturday evenings that intoxication can be seen in all its bestiality, for it is then that the workers have just received their wages and go out for enjoyment at rather earlier hours than on other days of the week. On Saturday evenings the whole working class streams from the slums into the main streets of the town. On such an evening in Manchester I have seldom gone home without seeing many drunkards staggering in the road or lying helpless in the gutter. … It is easy to see the consequences of widespread drunkenness – the deterioration of personal circumstances, the catastrophic decline in health and morals, the breaking up of homes.

Such fear over excessive drinking resulted in a reformist and modernizing bourgeois project that sought to affect the physical redevelopment of the city in order to improve industrial productivity and generate markets where disposable income was spent (responsibly) on goods and services (Becker 1966; Thompson 1967; Malcolmson 1973; Sennett 1977; Frisby 2001). Alongside religious concerns of the middle-classes regarding the piety of the lower-classes and a view that immorality dominated urban life, paternalistic concerns to improve the education, health and recreation pursuits of the working classes ensured that attempts to curtail excessive drinking were central to political and popular debate (Miller 1958; Hagan 1977; Bakhtin 1984; Stallybrass and White 1986; Malcolmson 1973; Rojek 1995). Bourgeois attempts to banish working-class consumption cultures from central urban spaces and places led to regulation, urban master planning, licensing laws, planning guidelines and formal policing all targeted at working-class drinking cultures, which were seen and a source of social vice, moral decline and as inhibiting industrial productivity (Cunningham 1980; Harring 1983; Cohen 1997). This reordering was underwritten by the moral logic of 'civilizing' that marked the regulation of drinking (see Valentine 1998).

For example, one of the most famous public debates concerning alcohol consumption emerged via the spatial metaphors of Gin Lane (a place of immoral behaviour – particularly by women – violence, slum life, disorder and potential revolution), and Beer Street (a place of joviality, business success, progress, modern civilized streets, houses and shops. While the favoured drink of the working classes was gin, which was cheap and plentiful, beer was considered to be a healthier alternative. Gin became central to middle-class anxieties over working class drunkenness, morality and fear of the unruly crowds (see O'Mally and Valverde 2004). The so-called gin palaces were a genuine product of the industrial revolution, where industrialized production techniques allowed high-alcohol content distilled spirits to be served to customers, shortening the inebriation process as well as the time drinkers stayed at the bar (see McAndrew and Edgerton 1969).

However, although conceptualization of the rationalization of industrialized modern urban life – the development of city centres, spatial segregation and a civilizing process relating to urban drinking and public space – provides a valuable vision of urban change there is undoubtedly a tendency to oversimplify their proliferation and impact. For example, while such broad-brush typologies that characterize the relationship between drinking and the development of the modern city provide a useful generalizable template (one that provides neat connections between, for example, the proliferation of Fordist production and consumption cultures, the success of middle-class crusades, and the social and spatial control of drinking), understanding of the relationship between the specific contexts of the people and places that are central to these practices and processes has been under-developed (Savage and Warde 1993). Moreover, the social relations and cultural practices and processes that surround drinking have generally been ignored. This denies that industrialized capital accumulation, bourgeois political control, the suppression of unruly working-class leisure activities, and the political, economic, social, cultural and physical redevelopment of the city was differentially and discursively constructed in different places at different times (Miles and Paddison 1998).

Indeed, Monkkonen (1981) describes an interesting case study of the early modern American city represented as being disorderly, violent, noisy and chaotic, and argues that attempts to 'civilize' city centres and central neighbourhoods were undermined by the availability of public transport and a concentration of drinking establishments. Monkkonen (1981, 540) suggests that the city of the late-nineteenth and early-twentieth centuries can be characterized by 'relatively intense use of public space by people of all classes' and that that bourgeois control over drinking, particularly at night time was never fully established in city centres. In the modern city, the large numbers of people from different social groups, converging from different parts of the city, ensured that drunkenness and disorder was a constant feature of urban life and public space. Monkkonen (1981) elaborates this position by discussing arrest rates for public drunkenness, in twenty-two American cities between 1860 and 1920. Despite statistical sources identifying a general decline in arrests over the period, Monkkenon shows that some cities (such as San Francisco, St Louis, Buffalo and Louisville) saw consistent growth in arrests for drunkenness and a further nine cities also showed increases at various times throughout this period. He also challenges the picture provided by such statistics by pointing to political concerns and associated changing legal definitions (and different policing strategies in each location) as a better explanation of increases/decreases in drunkenness in specific cities. Similar, conceptualization of the ways in which political concern around alcohol and drunkenness led to increased policing of alcohol in UK cities, in order define, measure and represent 'problem drinking' are shown to be underpinned by specific political, economic, social and cultural geographies. Beckingham (2008) shows that in 1878, Liverpool was depicted as most drunken city in England and describes the geographical imaginations relating to Liverpool as a city represented as rife with illegal drunkenness – a city 'on the margins' and 'out of control'.

Similar arguments are made about our case study city. For example, Holliday and Jayne (2000) highlight how historic representations of drinking in Stoke-on-Trent in the late eighteen and nineteenth century over emphasize social divisions and gloss over the complex mixing of classes, ages and genders in central urban areas via alcohol consumption (Holliday and Jayne 2000). In the 'alcohol-drenched potteries' (Edwards 1997, 25) Holliday and Jayne show how alcohol-related disorder and related social problems were a prominent element of political debate and everyday life in the city. The late eighteenth century saw a rapid rise in the number of places to buy alcohol. For example, in 1850 there were over 800 alcohol outlets and in 1857 a magistrate concluded that between 80–90 per cent of all crimes were related to drink (despite relatively low levels of actual arrests for drink related crimes). However, unlike elsewhere in the UK, the Temperance movement in The Potteries was small, fragmented and only had limited success in influencing local politics and social life. One of the key issues relating to the relative failings of the Temperance movements was the lack of a dominant middle-class and reformist agenda, but also the weakness of paternalistic activity amongst local industrialists, the local authority, the church and other bodies. The pottery owners and other local industrialists were slow to end practices such as paying workers in pubs, stamping down on absenteeism and on-the job drinking.

Similarly, public debates at the time represented an understanding that the poor quality of health and work-life for people in The Potteries and associated social problems were so acute that drinking was an understandable response to the living conditions in the city. Indeed, political ineffectuality, poor working conditions, low pay, unpaid holidays, and the availability of cheap alcohol ensured that rowdy and drunken behaviour dominated the city's streets. Moreover, the leisure opportunities for the population of Stoke-on-Trent were overwhelmingly dominated by excessive drinking, which perhaps explains the wide-held attitude of 'a picturesque, muscular, breezy old chap, a packer, at Powell's potbank, who, when asked why he regularly got drunk on the weekend, answered that it would not be weekend if he did not get drunk (*Evening Sentinel* 12/1/1978).

In 1896 a report in the *Evening Sentinel* suggested that in Stoke-on-Trent City Centre; 'The state of crown bank ... after dark is a scandal and a disgrace. The spirit vaults which thickly stud the border of the square were nightly filled with most abandoned characters ... whose discordant shouts, obscene gestures and brutal violence often made the place a perfect pandemonium'. However, alongside this depiction of alcohol-related disorder are contemporary accounts of the 'The Monkey Run', a circuit walk of the city centre streets by thousands of people which took place around the theatres, cinema and the concentration of pubs on Friday and Saturday nights. The monkey run offered (mainly) young people the opportunity to promenade around the city centre, enjoying the crowds, and the chance to 'see and be seen'. Descriptions of this turn of the century 'pub crawl' conflicts with visions of a night-time economy dominated by drunken disorder and violence, highlighting how alcohol, and a 'big night out' were enjoyed by many residents. Such contrasting representations have obvious resonances with contemporary concerns about alcohol and city life that will be returned to later. However, a key point to draw from this evidence is that despite political and popular concerns over 'out-of control' violent and disorderly cities, is that large numbers of people engaged in and enjoyed alcohol consumption as an integral part of urban life.

In theorizing everyday drinking practices Mary Douglas importantly challenges simplistic visions of alcohol as a social and medical problem. In the book *Constructive Drinking* (1987), Douglas sought to overcome the 'pathological' medicalized conceptualization that had dominated popular and academic discourses concerning alcohol and introduced a more 'neutral', but nonetheless critically productive 'anthropological' approach. Douglas argued that literatures concentrating on the physical effects of alcohol on the body and on issues such as the amount of working days lost to alcohol because of absenteeism were abstract at both at an individual and social level. However, the conception of alcohol as a 'social problem' (supported by medical discourse) nonetheless helped to underpin rational urban planning and fuelled the temperance movement's attempt to eradicate drinking from the nineteenth century city.

In following Mary Douglas, geographer James Kneale focuses on pub life, urban change and public space in various cities across the UK during the nineteenth century (also see McAndrew and Edgerton 1969; Giround 1975; Clarke 1983). Kneale (2004) looks at the social relations of 'drunken geographies', utilizing Mass Observation research material collected from 1937 to 1948. Mass Observation was part of a wider documentary movement in the UK, Europe and the US aimed to rejuvenate a public sphere corrupted by unrepresentative government, a biased Press and by advertising. In January 1936, Mass Observations recruited amateur observers to complete diary entries, collect newspapers cuttings and professional observers carried out covert and overt participation (Kneale 1991, 2001, 2004). One of the central reasons that the Mass Observation project was undertaken was due to a contemporary dissatisfaction with the way in which drinking was reported by official statistics, and also a concern that official measures to curb drunkenness failed to grasp the experience and context of drinking. This was underpinned by a view that the pub was a complex social space in which class and gender identities were constituted and reproduced. Mass Observation studies of pub life were undertaken in Bolton, Blackpool, Plymouth, Liverpool and Fulham.

Kneale described how experiences of drunkenness were learnt through socialization, arguing that drinkers did not consider that they were involved in a transgressive practice, but rather that drinking was simultaneously about being part of the community and also about being a good customer. Pubs were considered by their patrons to be spaces for relatively intimate social relations, and encapsulated within this are associations of drunkenness with commensality, trust and reciprocity that encouraged a relaxation of inhibitions. Kneale also shows that rooms within pubs were strictly gendered; the vault and taproom were masculine spaces, while the lounge or parlour were dominated by couples or mixed groups. Kneale quotes Bakhtin (1984) and suggests pub life and drinking was a form of dialogue, an engagement that held out the offer of diversity and heterogeneity. Beyond the pub, one of the most important features of the Mass Observation research related to drinking and public space. The formation of crowds of people, drunk and not-so drunk, engaging with one another and with other users of public space was seen as a key feature of drunken behaviour. In particular, the promenading of people (like the Monkey run in Stoke-on-Trent) after closing time, in large but often temporary groups of people was shown to be a key component of urban drinking.

Mass Observation also described the symbolic importance of drinking noting that drinking was a way of creating and transforming social relationships between people, via trust, reciprocity and a relaxing of formal social relations. For example, the working-class drinking practice of 'rounds' and 'treating' one another reproduced social ties and obligations, and hence drinking was seen to have played an important role in making connections between people. Drink was equated with social worth, trust, reciprocity and fraternity. Drunkenness was bound up with group intoxication, and was described by Mass Observation as a social phenomenon of self-liberation from the weekly work routine and time-discipline, just as Engels had described in the quote at the beginning of this chapter, allowed people to break down social inhibitions. It was also argued that sobriety and drunkenness were controlled through social hierarchies and particularly through the guidance of older drinkers. So, even though drunkenness created particular bonds of sociality between drinkers and a temporary suspension of particular social divisions, there were still social norms to adhere to. Despite the growing popularity of non-alcoholic drinks such as tea, coffee, and milk, and the proliferation of 'drinkable' water supplies for the first time, in working-class areas where drinking was engrained in everyday life and forms of sociability, curbing excessive drinking proved to be a great challenge to middle-class reformists (see Burnett 1999).

Moreover, Kneale argues that during the nineteenth century public debate surrounding the construction of public space was bound up with sensitivity to the social problems associated with the conviviality of drinking and the role of the drink trade. Kneale shows that temperance documents between 1856 and 1914 trace two different geographical imaginations of public space. He suggests that a customary sense of public space based on drink as a form of gift exchange (which symbolized strong bonds of reciprocity) was becoming marginalized. This was defined by the political tenets of liberal democracy, adhering to the characteristics of the public sphere where individuals are aware of their responsibilities as citizens. Temperance was underpinned by idealized characteristics of the public sphere as a place of inclusive sober citizenship, and certain groups and activities had to be excluded. Drink and the drink trade were thus defined as problematic and geographical and scientific knowledge played their part in legislating and guiding state action. However, such notions of public space were contested via practices in everyday life such as alcohol consumption. As such, despite dominant middle-class agendas and the powerful temperance movement, bourgeois political control, the suppression of unruly working-class leisure activities, and the redevelopment of the city due to fears over the 'evils of drink' were differentially constructed and experienced in different ways in specific cities Miles and Paddison 1998).

Binge City? Alcohol, Drinking, Drunkenness and Contemporary Urban Life

Over the past thirty years, many cities have re-invented themselves as sites of consumption (Zukin 1998; Hannigan 1998; Jayne 2005). This has been bound up with political and socio-cultural change associated with Fordism, Post-Fordism and neo-Fordism (Kumar 1995); changes in the local state and the rise of the entrepreneurial city (Hall and Hubbard 1998); a decline in extractive and industrial manufacturing and a move towards a more service based, cultural and 'symbolic' economy, which includes the support of leisure and the night-time economy

(Lash and Urry 1994; Lovatt and O'Connor 1995; Scott 2000). Alongside these changes has been the increasing importance of consumption, especially in relation to market segmentation, gentrification and branding, as well as increased globalization and corporatization (Featherstone 1991; Klein 2000). It is in this context, that alcohol consumption has become part of the regeneration strategies of urban areas which have sought new avenues for wealth creation via the entertainment economy. As David Bell notes (2005, 26), 'the experience economy of cities or districts' generally includes the provision of 'drinkatainment', based around drinking attractions (and other contemporary landmarks, including theatres and restaurants) such as themed bars and pubs ranging from staged authenticity provided by Irish theme pubs to Soviet styled vodka bars.

There have been a number of attempts to conceptualize the political-economic, social, cultural and spatial practices and processes bound up with the relationship between drinking and contemporary urban change. However, in essence there remains (in our cities today) the kind of dualistic set of arguments that were noted as surrounding alcohol, drinking in drunkenness of the late eighteenth and early nineteenth century. For example, books by Paul Chatterton and Robert Hollands, *Urban Nightscapes: Youth Cultures, Pleasure, Spaces and Corporate Power* (2003); Dick Hobbs et al. *Bouncers: Violence and Governance in the Night-time Economy* (2003) and Simon Winlow and Steve Hall's volume *Violent Night: Urban Leisure and Contemporary Culture* (2006) have sought to frame debates and develop theoretical arguments regarding the night-time economy and drinking. These writers have considered; who and what is involved in producing nightlife spaces (for example, designing, marketing, selling, property markets, corporate strategies etc); who and what is involved in regulating them (for example laws and legislation, surveillance, entrance points, codes of conduct); who and what are the consumers and consumption practices that are present in the consumption practices that surround them (for example, lived experience, perceptions and stereotypes).

This work has usefully concluded that urban nightlife is constructed through a number of contradictory tendencies towards both deregulation and (re) regulation, and the twin imperatives of fun and disorder. On the one hand, during the weekends and evenings, city streets host large number of young revellers intent on having fun, spending money, drug taking, dancing, encountering and subversion. This is an economy of pleasure, and the 24 hour city becomes the vehicle for economic growth, profit generation and entrepreneurialism. However, while the financial success of drinking has stimulated further demand for its deregulation, the night-time continues to be heavily influenced by Fordist concerns for tighter regulation, social control and zoning, due to lingering moral panics and fear of disorder. The city, especially at night is shown to be contradictory – simultaneously conflictual and segregated, commodified and sanitized, saturated by both emotion (enhanced through alcohol, drugs, dance, sex, encounter) and rational elements (planning, surveillance and policing) – and that such tensions are not always easy to understand and reconcile.

For example, in comparing the drinking 'quarters' of four European cities – Soho and Covent Garden (London), Temple Bar (Dublin), Nyhaven (Copenhagen) and the Hackerscher Market (Berlin) Roberts et al. (2006) usefully argue that the UK governments licensing policy has been developed via a 'simplistic and one-dimensional link ... made between a *laissez-faire* attitude to re-regulation of licensing hours and a 'continental' or 'sensible' drinking culture (Roberts et al. 2009, 1109). In doing so the research highlights a number of interconnected issues such as planning controls, licensing systems, policing, density of venues, type of venues (vertical/seated drinking, restaurants etc), CCTV provision and so on in order to consider how alcohol related violence and disorder play out in different ways in each location.

While making a valuable argument Roberts et al. (2006), nonetheless fall into the trap of accepting rather than critiquing the use of terms such as European/ continental drinking and the implicit binge-drinking British 'other'. As such, while highlighting how issues surrounding noise, disorder and violence are differently constructed in each case study area the argument does not move beyond a generalizable depiction of drinking practices in each location and fails to consider the diversity of drinking experiences in those places (see Jayne et al. 2006; Latham 2003). Moreover, in justifying their case study choice 'on the supposition that drinking habits of northern Europe were more comparable with Britain than Mediterranean or predominantly wine-drinking cultures' (Roberts et al. 2006, 1109), the authors explicitly fail to unpack an overly simplistic categorization of drinking practices associated with these particular national 'stereotypes' (see Jayne et al. 2008b). This is further exemplified in the choice of comparable case study areas (drinking quarters, tourist locations, capital cities) while being understandable does nothing to begin to represent the diversity of drinking places and cultures within and beyond those cities.

Despite contemporary corporate success in dominating urban life, conflicts around the way in which drinking plays an important role in everyday life can thus be argued to be as high-profile today as it was in the late eighteenth and early nineteenth centuries. Indeed, currently, the long standing 'moral panic' concerning the 'evils of drink' has resurfaced in the UK around city-centre drinking cultures, initially through concern over 'lager louts' and more recent in figure of 'binge drinkers' (Gofton 1990; Hobbs et al. 2000; Lister et al. 2000). Thus, in the midst of urban regeneration initiatives that have developed night-time economies based around new consumption landscapes characterized by hybrid corporate cafe/bar/club venues (that are argued to usurp and commercialize public space) concerns about alcohol-fuelled disorder, drunken brawling, public sex acts, and litter from take-away food wrapping strewn across streets, have emerged. *Violent Night* by Winlow and Hall (2006, 1) maintains this trend and in particular seeks to offer a theoretical perspective that moves beyond 'a romanticizing of consumer capitalism, and compulsion to avoid moral judgements ... gloss over the serious problems besetting young people ... [by considering the relationship between alcohol consumption and] anxiety, drugs, violence, suicide, loss of traditional forms of identity, consumer pressure and so on'. Winlow and Hall suggests that we are experiencing epochal change and disjuncture from the past, and that alcohol related violence and disorder is bound up young people seeking to 'make sense of their place' in the contemporary world. The erosion of traditional class based relationships, improved educational opportunities in parallel with a low waged economy, the decline in union power and the emergence of a permanently excluded underclass are shown to be the root of alcohol related violence in the night-time economy. *Violent Night* argues that young people these days – dominated by consumer culture with its tight grip on their identities and emotional lives and its modelling of youth culture to suit the needs of neo-capitalism – are literally hitting back.

In contrast other theorists have argue urban change and regeneration is a contested process that does not necessarily lead to decline or the demise of older-established spaces, identities or lifestyles. This suggests the need for a closer reading of spaces affected by gentrification in order to explore the emergence of particular kinds of social practices associated with specific instances of urban change (Latham 2003; Bell and Binnie 2005). In sum, scratching the surface appearance of urban transformation allows depiction not of a homogenized, purified set of spaces and experiences but something more complicated and contested. As such, political economy accounts of alcohol and urban life tend to over-emphasize the tendencies to obliterate local distinctiveness and reproduce blandscapes in cities throughout the world. While there is indeed a proliferation of standardization through regeneration in different cities (in terms of the serial reproduction of dominant motifs of regeneration schemes), the inter-play of pre-existing landscapes and lifestyles with those promoted by regeneration and gentrification, suggests that drink and regeneration combine in complex ways (see Bell and Binnie 2005 who make the same point about urban foodscapes). Far than being homogenized by regeneration projects, drinking is a varied activity constructed through diverse practices and experiences.

This point is elaborated in detail by Alan Latham (2003), who shows that an urban renaissance of Western industrialized urbanity has been robustly criticized by political economists who identify that the contemporary city is riddled with social division. Latham's (2003, 1709) ethnographic study of two streets in Auckland, New Zealand uncovers a public culture that is underpinned by tolerance diversity and creative energy, with a mixing of post-industrial lifestyles, with sexually polymorphous and industrial male public cultures that inhabit hotels and pubs. He suggests that there is a mix of 'self-consciously worldly spaces' and traditional pubs, where 'groups are mixed sex and not infrequently of openly mixed sexualities, and if people get drunk that is rarely the main purpose of the evening but rather a rather pleasant side effect of the night's socializing' (2003, 1712). In these terms Latham (2003, 1719) depicts cities as 'enormous machines for the generation of connections between the unexpected and the unexceptional'. This suggests that cities are on-going experiments into how people of different backgrounds, incomes, wealth and values can live together. Latham acknowledges that while this can produce divisions, it can also produce new connection, hybrids and unexpected meanings. He describes a situation in Auckland that does not conform to a model of gentrification like that posited by Zukin (and many later writers), but a mixing of vernacular and gentrified, and a convivial ecology, which can be seen to spill into the streets generating 'new solidarities and new collectivities' and a greater sense of belonging (Latham 2003, 1719).

Latham's depictions contrast markedly not only to the work of Chatterton and Hollands, Hobbs et al., Winlow and Hall and others but also with ethnographic research undertaken in the relatively near neighbour city of Melbourne. Lindsay (2005), for example, while noting market and social segmentation and branding, did not consider the impact of the emergence of new pubs and clubs on the public spaces that conjoin commercial venues to have radically altered long standing street cultures bound up with alcohol consumption. In a similar vein, Morean (2005, 25) shows that in Japan the branding and clustering of venues in specific localities means that 'different kinds of drinking establishments tend to be found together in different parts of every city'. While this would appear to produce drinking districts aimed at market segments such as politicians, media professionals, young people, students and academics and so on Morean described a complex mixing of social groups within, surrounding and between these venues or locations.

What becomes clear in these competing critiques of urban milieu is that both political-economy and studies that are more socially, culturally and spatially detailed and nuanced must be employed if our understanding of the relationship between urban life and alcohol, drinking, and drunkenness are to be advanced. Such a synthesis is important not only in terms of an academic research agenda, but is also fundamental to guiding urban policy making and planning. For example, there are ambiguities that surround policy making, policing and urban drinking. Constructions of public space are argued on the one hand to be bound up with increased commercialization, and the exclusion (of non-consumers) which intensifies and deepens social divisions (Hannigan 1998). In these terms public spaces therefore represent a framing of a particular vision of the social life of the city and 'acceptable' cultural practices underpinned by ideas of regeneration formulated around an assessment of threats to security, and concerns to domesticate public space, manage diversity, and reduce the 'risky' mixing of different social groups by the new middle classes (Merrifield 2000). In a similar vein, Atkinson (2003) describes the gentrification of public space as being underpinned by control and empowerment, fostering fearful rather than inclusive public spaces and exclusionary policies – a process he describes as 'domestication by cappuccino' – and which has contributed to (and been underpinned by) the proliferation of bourgeois café bars, restaurants, delicatessens and so on.

In these terms drinking in our cities raises the idea that drinkers are consumers who are often being badly behaved and do not conform to discourses of polite, civilized and cosmopolitan urbanity. Hand in hand with privatization and security, bouncers, CCTV, wardens, anti-begging strategies, strategies to discourage rough sleepers and skateboard-proof street furniture has been a proliferation of 'drinkatainment' and the presence of socially diverse drunken consumers. Thus, while drinkatainment is founded on an 'entertainment experience economy [that] themes excitement and enjoyment, [this then also comes under siege from] the presence of drunken crowds ... [and which] (re)constitutes the space as one that is controlled decontrol threatening to get out of hand' (Bell and Binnie 2005, 28). Similarly, the presence of pavement side café bar and restaurant tables and chairs and, 'homeless people supping cheap cans of larger or just sitting in the sun', is also an example of social mixing and the co-presence of different groups (Bell and Binnie 2005, 29).

Key to attempts to eradicate anti-social behaviour has been zero tolerance policing (ZTP), initiated in cities throughout the world in order to address the presence of unwanted social groups and exclude both illegal activity and 'bad behaviour' (Belina and Helms 2003). Zero tolerance policing is thus a component of political and economic restructuring and is linked to the requirements of urban competitiveness and image promotion (Hall and Hubbard 1998). This idea is most effectively developed by Neil Smith in his depiction of the 'Revanchist City' (1996). Smith describes the interrelationships between urban restructuring and an ideology of revanchism as 'a blend of revenge and reaction' (1998, 1). This discourse depicts the city as being stolen from the white middle classes by all sorts of minorities, and crime is a central marker. However, Raco (2003) agues that we should be wary of generalizing the outcomes of the privatization of space, for example, in the UK, ZTP has developed at the same time as debates about more 'compassionate' ideas about policing 'without policing' and the development of neighbourhood and city-centre wardens. According to Body-Gendrot (2000), such policies are part of a broader neo-liberal move to devolved decentralized government that leads towards discretionary policy-making which has targeted local communities as a way of dealing with urban violence. As such, while being embedded in broader institutional discourses and practices, the implementation of security measures has been mediated, in part, by the local socio-political and cultural relations. Raco (2003, 1840) argues that 'we must think carefully about how access to public space is changing'.

For example, in the UK, Hobbs (2003) depicts the high percentage of drinking related violent crime over the weekends, around 30 per cent within or near licensed premises; of which 68 per cent between 2100 hours to 0300 hours, peaking around 2300 hours. However, political responses to tackle such violence has focused around plans to extend licensing hours, in order to stagger pub, bar and club closing times and hence avoiding the 2300 hours outpouring of drinkers onto the streets. Such policy making is undertaken in the context of an appreciation that the cultural economy of drinking is an important generator of wealth and urban reputation and that policing is a delicate balancing act on one the one hand maintaining order and control, and on the other not stifling the very conditions that attract so many consumers (see Hobbs et al. 2003).

Hobbs shows police interventions into urban drinking and drunkenness are focused on discouraging or intervening in violent public disorder policed through swift, labour-intensive responses and a swarming of units. It is clear then that despite the increasing crime that there is little ZTP related with drinking and drunkenness but rather targeted responses take place where personal safety or where public order offences are committed. A further measure widely used in the UK is the filming of revellers (by police officers with hand help video cameras), initiated as a 'calming measure', in an attempt to remind individuals of their behavioural responsibilities, before any offences are committed. Indeed given that such anti-social behaviour (unlike other 'quality of life offences') seems to be a very sociable activity undertaken by active consumers, it is clear that the police are reluctant to intervene in the drunkenness of active citizens of the consumer society.

Moreover, there is also balancing act bound up with implicit understandings that alcohol plays a central role in many people's non-work activities and thus to a large degree enables more productive workers. In these terms alcohol consumption continues to be a problem that needs 'to be solved' by political and social reform in specific ways, focused on specific bodies and emotions in specific spaces (see Jayne et al. 2006; 2008). Thus drinking has been depicted as a problem that can, at least be partially, attended to by legislative change, but also as being central to attempts to achieve an urban renaissance (see Jayne et al. 2006; 2008a). In particular it has been young people (and particularly highly 'sexualized' women), drinking 'new' types of drinks in (non-traditional) vertical drinking establishments that characterize problematic drinking cultures. However, at 'street level', violence and disorder has been shown to be of minimal concern, particularly in the context of the large numbers of people who enjoy drinking alcohol in cities (see Valentine et al. 2007a). Indeed, beyond the rhetoric of politicians, senior police officers and National Health Service officials which signals the drain of resources that policing and alcohol consumption entails, admissions by 'on the ground' police officers show that the police are reluctant to engage with individuals drinking unless they are a harm to themselves, others or property (Valentine et al. 2007b).

Indeed, a cursory review of the proportion of crime involving alcohol as a mediating factor shows high levels of drink related crime in The Potteries. Such figures reflect broader trends within the UK. Out of 354 local authority areas in the UK Stoke-on-Trent is ranked in the top 10 per cent for alcohol related recorded crime and alcohol related violent offences (North West Public Health Observatory, Local Alcohol Profiles for England, 2006). However, both political and popular debate has thrown up some interesting contradictions that we seek to investigate here – in simple terms – if the streets are plagued with anti-social behaviour and violence why do so many people regularly spend their leisure time drinking in public places? How do people experience, perceive and manage the risks and benefits associated with public drinking and how do these contrast with official depictions, management and policing of people's drinking?

Nonetheless, at the level of policy formation and associated policing techniques, the relationship between drinking and disorder appears to be quite clear – excessive drinking is 'out of control', and measures to stop the further expansion of the night-time economy are necessary as are increased resources to tackle the problem. Indeed, some commentators have suggested that the ability of the police to intervene in relation to the problems of urban drinking and drunkenness is hampered by a lack of resources. Thus it is claimed that the police can only react to specific incidents, swarming units (a labour-intensive response) to deal with flashpoints (Hobbs et al. 2000) rather than develop preventative policing strategies. As a senior police officer in Staffordshire Police (Stoke-on-Trent Division) suggested:

> the situation with regards to violent crime particularly in the city centre environments is, is very similar whether it be Stoke-on-Trent, whether it be Cardiff, whether it be Manchester, whether it be Liverpool, and you know, Blackpool. I've visited most of those areas to compare the set up, shall we say in Manchester and Blackpool to what it's like in Stoke-on-Trent and there are many similarities in terms of the problems that you'd find on the streets of Manchester and Blackpool as you'd find in Stoke-on-Trent ... You know it's issues of young people who've got disposable income, who, who are tempted by drinks promotions and who are binge drinking that is then leading on to problems, you know, intensely dense areas and people coming out of premises at night, flashpoints and so on and so on and so on, and we try to put some strategies in place to try and minimize the effects of all of those, with some success, but there's considerable more work to be done. [Later he continued...] And if we're going to, you know if we're going to keep investing in the city centre to get more and more and more premises in there that have got licenses, that will mean that we will need to increase the Policing in there [edit].

However, the broad range of measures and approaches utilized by 'on the ground' police officers in Stoke-on-Trent suggests that there is a mismatch between the policing rhetoric of senior officers and the actual policing of drunkenness on the streets. Indeed, conversations held with low ranking police officers on the street show a very different attitude towards policing drunkenness than that depicted by senior officers, as these quotations from three different junior officers illustrate:

> You don't want to arrest someone who is drunk and disorderly, it's just too much bother, you want to be sending them on their way with no trouble.

> It's not bad ... as some places. There are about ten of us on and ten in support.

> It's a bit rowdy and there are high spirits but there's not that much trouble – a lot of stuff about the violence associated with binge drinking is media hype – its not that people don't drink too much and are badly behaved but its only low level stuff ... the streets aren't out of control – the actual arrest rates are low.

Behaviour considered as 'anti-social' at a policy level clearly is for a large proportion of respondents considered as 'having a good time', indeed police at street level suggested that where people's drunkenness does not pose a serious threat to personal or public safety they are reluctant to intervene unnecessarily. Zero-tolerance policing is not applied to managing public drinking.

Moreover, while we must bear in mind Leyshon's (2005, 2008) depictions of complex unequal social relations surrounding drinking, most respondents describe alcohol consumption positively in terms of emotional and embodied senses of 'belonging' (this will be returned to in Chapter 7 – also see Holloway et al. 2008, 2009; Valentine et al. 2009; Jayne et al. 2010). Indeed, although some respondents suggested that you could feel 'out of place' in venues by appearing to be too old or too young, or by visiting venues they didn't know well; and while others feared gendered, racist or homophobic comments and violence, most respondents talked about being feeling 'at home' in a range of places because of alcohol consumption. Indeed, experiences and attitudes to the risks associated with violence and disorder are illuminating. Only one or two people, interviewed in-depth had personally been involved in violent incidents and while many had witnessed scuffles and fighting the overwhelming responses followed the lines of: It is clear from such comments that while violence is understood to be a problem, people mobilize various strategies of avoidance and vigilance in order to ensure personal safety.

In our study respondents of different ages, genders and social backgrounds thus talk of drinking predominantly as being related to particular characteristics and functions of a night out, rather than drinking as an accelerator of violence. This includes younger people, escaping the pressures and time constraints of work in order to spend time with their friends 'out and about' or young families who can spend time away from their children and let their hair down. Older people talked similarly about the 'occasion' of a night out, the 'performance' of getting dressed up, the heightened sociability and the relaxed sociability offered by drinking. It is clear that all that is involved in the 'going out-ness' of a drinking experience – the drama, the dressing up, the occupation of public space, of 'proper' streets and public squares and statues and the presence of crowds involved in 'improper' activities – is of central importance to a 'big night out' (see Hubbard 2002).

In these terms, Merrifield (2000) rightly argues then, that urban space is kept alive by such practices. Indeed as Laurier and Philo (2004, 4) suggest, the 'rumbustiousness of the crowd, as [well as] the self-interest of the individual are transformed into a new kind of sociality', and that places such as café's (or in terms of the topic at hand drinking establishments) provide space and support for communal life in the city. In contrast to Hubbard's (2003) depiction of patronage of suburban multiplexes as an assessment of riskless risk, or as Hannigan (1998) suggests, 'quasi-liminal' experiences that allow an avoidance of 'urban other' by going to unthreatening leisure and cleansed urban space, drinking is a practice that appears to go hand-in-hand with negotiating and navigating the risky city. Moreover, with urban restructuring ensuring that pubs, clubs and bars (like shops) are now often densely concentrated, allowing consumers to browse and, in terms of the pub/bar, to promenade, drinkatainment is a practice bound up with drunkenness and loss of personal and social inhibitions. Perhaps, however, it is precisely because of the perceived risk and risk taking involved in urban drinking which ensures that it is a collective and public activity. Drinking, described by Latham as a mixing of social groups on the street, is then a collectivity that is risky risk, but in urban space drunkenness and the collectivity that is part of this, (despite the incidents of violence) is clearly attractive. Understanding and balancing these tensions is of course a challenge to policy makers.

This ambiguity surrounding public space is well established by Thomas (2002) who in discussing an interesting case study from South East Asia identifies changes in the nature of public space in Hanoi, Vietnam. Thomas shows how economic and social transformations have paved the way for a dramatic change in the way in which streets, pavements and markets are experienced and imagined. She argues that an emerging bustling street life has further destabilized state control and struggle for meaning in public space. It is in this context that Thomas shows how public spaces are attracting large numbers of people for supposedly non-political activities, but which are being labelled as transgressive and condemned by the state. The consumption of alcohol, young people racing motorbikes, religious meetings, football crowds, and outpourings of grief during the funeral processions of national pop stars are just some of the ways in which behaviour in public space is causing political concern (Thomas 2002).

In a similar vein, Edensor (2006) describes the development of the waterfront area in the city of Port Louis in Mauritius, noting how the 'Keg and Marlin' pub has provided a new place for local people to mingle, overcoming strict racial and religious segregation. The pub opens up the possibility of communal participation and is 'a convivial venue for alcohol-fuelled loud talk and expressive behaviour, modes of conduct that transgress ordinary constraints of family and community oriented social practice' (Edensor 2006, 17). Elsewhere, Hunt et al. (2005) show that street drinking by gangs of ethnic young men in San Francisco offers economically, cultural and spatially marginalized people the opportunity to visibly contribute to urban street life. Similarly, Altay (2008) describes 'Minibar' which emerges around and between buildings in Ankara, Turkey, where young people, not being able to afford bars and clubs, take advantage of pavements and low masonry walls 'to hang out' and drink alcohol.

Such examples show how the use of public space for everyday activities such as drinking is a catalyst for crowd formation. For example, Thomas (2002) utilizes the work of Habermas (1974) to argue that gathering together to exchange information and ideas, allowed a 'public sphere' to develop in much the same way as it did in Europe in the eighteenth century. Habermas argued that the growth of urban culture – eating, leisure and meeting places – fuelled the development of the public sphere. However, Miles' (2000) argument concerning young people's occupation of public space is perhaps useful here. Miles argues that young people's seemingly transgressive practices of hanging out at the mall, or on street corners, or skateboarding, have little to do with transgression and conflict but rather are an attempt to carve out a place for themselves in the city and to assert their identities as active participants in consumer society. Drinking and drunkenness should perhaps be considered in terms of the connectivities and belonging generated in public space, and as being grounded in pleasures, enjoyment and 'riskiness' of heterogeneous groups of people mixing in city spaces in ways that would not be acceptable, to them or city authorities, if the mediating factor of the consumption of alcohol in bars, pubs and other establishments, enabled drinkers to claim to be active citizens.

Conclusion

The relationship between sociability, alcohol consumption, drunkenness and urban life has been at the forefront of political, policy and popular debates for over two hundred years. During this time the working classes, women and young people have become central to concerns over city centres as violent, disorderly and out of control. Despite such representations, large numbers of people continue to enjoy the conviviality of drinking and drunkenness in commercial venues and public spaces within our cities. In these terms it is important that theorists begin to move beyond considering alcohol and city life in the kind of dualistic manner outlined in this chapter. To this end it is vital that future research seeks to unpack the discursive and differential construction of (un)problematic drinking and associated behaviours, as well as seeking greater understanding of the conflicts and tensions that arise around alcohol, drinking and drunkenness for different social groups, in different urban spaces and places in cities throughout the world.

Chapter 2
The Countryside

Writing that considers alcohol, drinking and drunkenness in rural areas, although less voluminous than writing on the city, has sought to engage with the political, economic, social, cultural and spatial practices and processes that constitute ideological constructions of 'the countryside'. In broad terms the rural landscape is commonly portrayed as an idyllic place to grow up (Bunce 1994; Short 1991). This imagining of the rural has as Kraack and Kenway (2002, 146) describe both 'aesthetic and moral components'. The aesthetic component refers to the way that 'the rural' is commonly understood to be a picturesque, natural physical environment, characterized by trees, fields and open space. The moral component alludes to the way that rural communities are stereotyped as close-knit, harmonious environments, where residents can live out a simple/pure existence free from the stress, dangers and corruptions of urban life (Ward 1990). In this chapter we draw on these arguments to show that while 'the rural' has historically been characterized as the antithesis of the urban, theorists considering alcohol consumption have begun to contribute to a more nuanced understanding of the relationship between the countryside and the city.

Theorizing Drinking in the Countryside

There is a growing body of writing that seeks to understand the place of alcohol, drinking and drunkenness in rural life. For example, anthropological studies that focus on rural areas in 'developing countries' have considered the relationship between the 'natural rhythms' of agricultural production and related constructions of masculinity and femininity. Men and women's relationship to farming via discourses of fertility and physical strength have been investigated in terms of the social rules that circulate around alcohol. Where drunkenness for men is celebrated as loosening everyday conscious states in order to make men more productive farmers, women's connection to nature is expressed through menstruation and childbirth. Around these stories, the times, amounts and types of drinks ascribed to gendered roles and rules have been considered (see De Garine and De Garine 2001; Gefou-Madianou 1992). For example, in rural Africa and Europe, writers have investigated the symbolic role of alcohol in terms of fertility. De Garine's (2001) study of tribal life in Cameroon presents a distinction between the role of beer in rituals and everyday life, where masculinity is constructed via different levels of drunkenness for different occasions when men can become drunk so that – 'he walks from the right to left, falls down, sometimes vomits and fights'. In a similar vein Papagaroufali (1992) describes how gender differences are played out in celebratory drinking practices in contemporary rural Greece where Ouzo is considered as a 'manly' drink, whereas women are supposed to favour fruit-flavoured liqueurs or 'sipping' beer and wine diluted with soft drinks.

Elsewhere in Europe gendered drinking has been shown to be bound up with specific rural spaces and places. Abad (2001) shows that in Spain, at different times of the year men drink throughout the day in public spaces in order to assure the fertility of the land and to ensure a productive harvest. In contrast women are only allowed to consume alcohol in public on feast days, or in secret while on trips to nearby towns. The relationship between gender and agricultural tradition is also present in the work of Bianquis-Gasser (1992), who in discussing the French region of Alsace, shows how drinking practices change at different points of the agricultural calendar. Alcohol consumption is associated with 'men's affairs', where men drink as a sacrament, often in cellars likened to a chapel – cold, vaulted, silent and dark. To achieve immortality men must drink deeply – they must loose their everyday conscious state, their mundane awareness. Women gain this status through childbirth and men by making and drinking wine.

The relationship between productivity is also considered by Peace (1992) who focuses on drinking and rural identity in Ireland. In this case, men's substantial drinking takes place in a small number of bars frequented by fishermen, where dramas and sagas around competitive fishing practices unfold. The men constantly move between bars in order to ensure the possibility of conversational encounters, to support camaraderie and to facilitate conflict. Such movement is important not only in terms of social cohesion but also in terms of securing work opportunities. In a similar vain, Campbell (2000) considers the performativity of gender in rural New Zealand, depicting 'conversational cockfighting' and disciplines of 'being able to hold your drink' – describing the pub as the last bastion of male camaraderie.

The place of men in the pub is also shown by Ní Laoire (2001) to be central to assertions of rural masculinity and marginalization in the face of the restructuring of the countryside. For example, Heley (2008) talks about the shifting terrain of rural pubs – and describes how a fraction of newcomers have tried to (re)create the typical English gentlemen (New Squires) that involves a nostalgic fiction of a provincial bygone age. Ales 'off the wood', tankards on the shelf, and dominance of an area of the pub known as 'the office' previously colonized by local framers is now a destination of choice for this new collective, aware of the historic role of this private bar. In a similar vein, Wolcott's (1974) description of African beer gardens in Bulawayom, Mar's (1987) study of Newfoundland longshoremen and Hansen's (1976) study of bars in Catalonia shows how 'freezing out' techniques are used in order to make people feel uncomfortable and assert particular masculine identities. Such writing is thus focused on considering constructions of hegemonic masculinity and the ways in which idealized local rural identities are legitimized around around alcohol consumption. This is taken further by Leyshon (2005, 2008) who describes the binaries of masculinity and femininity, and the trading of insults such as 'drinking like a girl' in rural England. Leyshon (2005) also considers bodily drinking performances and the ways in which gatherings of men were exclusive, hierarchical, homophobic and sexist, where men consume large amounts of alcohol without seeming drunk and by visibly and loudly occupying specific spaces in the pub.

Research has also focused on restructuring of the rural economy in terms of class conflict. In the UK, Hunt and Satterlee (1986) argue that that while 'the pub' can be a place where social groups occupy the same space, social barriers are also consolidated in these spaces. In particular, Hunt and Satterlee discuss the impact of urban life on the countryside via industrial re-structuring and middle-class incomers. Drawing on research in a Cambridgeshire village with seven pubs, the research shows how alcohol can enhance social solidarity as well as entrenching social demarcation and division. Working-class pubs were described as being the neighbourhoods' social centre, where round buying in intimate groups, or the pooling of money and drinking with offspring and kin were commonplace. Working-class pubs re-affirmed a cohesion that already existed, and incomers, if they lived on the 'right' estate would be gradually accepted, but as they didn't have a shared knowledge or historical connections with the locality and the pub, never fully accepted.

In contrast, drinking in middle-class pubs is shown to be focused on good fellowship and of being part of the 'right-set' of people. Within this process of forging 'belonging', Hunt (1991) describes particular discourses of public/private drinking and also 'civilizing' ideas that the working-class could learn from the middle-class drinking practices. Hunt's (1991) in-depth research focuses on a group of twenty six people, middle-class couples, who regularly meet up at the local pub particularly on weekends. Alongside 'their local' pub this group also visit restaurants, other nearby pubs and social events in the village, such as Conservative club, wine and cheese tasting, the football club annual dance and barbeques. Hunt highlights how round buying for everyone in the group was a key element in indicating disposable income and ritual affirmation status and belonging. However, unlike the working class pubs, the importance of maintaining social bonds via domestic drinking was vital to middle-class identity formation via a number of home rituals.

Firstly, then, were formal dinner parties, where guests take a bottle of wine (the host puts it in the kitchen to be drunk on another occasion) and are offered an aperitif (usually whisky or a gin and tonic) before dinner where specific wines are drunk with each course. Secondly, more informal dinner/lunch parties take place on Saturday afternoon after the pub closes and often include around a dozen people. Hunt describes drunken behaviour such as bike rides around the garden with obstacles, and other ball games such as croquet and football taking place usually after a large amount of alcohol has been drunk. As darkness fell, Hunt tells how the party tends to move into the house where loud music and dancing often led to performances such simulated 'falling over' pretending to be drunk and simulated sexual intercourse. Thirdly, at 'formal parties' guests dress in black tie and give the hosts a gift of flowers, chocolates or liqueurs, wine was given to the guests on arrival and throughout the night, finishing with the drinking of spirits. Similar stories are presented in rural Japan. However, Visser (1991, 189) shows at middleclass dinner parties, guests do not pour their own sake. Pouring is done by guests for each other, as a sign of social awareness and good will. Sake cups for dinner parties are small, so that service must constantly be repeated, and everyone must be on the watch for the chance to be neighbourly and fill somebody else's' cup.

Finally, the 'informal party' is a large gathering of up to fifty people. Guests contribute wine or large cans of beer to the party, and add these to the stock of alcohol already on display in the kitchen. Where guests contribute an expensive bottle of wine or spirits this was often discreetly hidden away by the guests to be found later. Guests are served with a drink of their choice on arrival and then expected to help themselves. Snacks and nibbles are provided but then hot sausage rolls and chilli con carne from a large pot are offered by the hosts. Guests socialize in small clusters throughout the evening and people 'circulate'. Most left at eleven o'clock but a core small groups stay until the early hours of the morning. In sum, Hunt (1991) summarizes these different social gatherings in terms of the degrees of hospitality related to levels of intimacy.

Hunt (1991) also highlights that at the informal lunch/dinner parties non-violent drunken behaviour is acceptable but at formal parties and dinner parties' drunken behaviour was not acceptable. The more formal the event the more formal practices of alcohol consumption, aperitifs, wine with each course and drunkenness is frowned upon. Indeed, Hunt (1991) tells the story of one guest who drank too much whisky before dinner, while initially being ignored by the other guests, was excused by his wife on the grounds that he was having a hard day at the office when he fell asleep and started to snore at the dinner table. In contrast, at more informal events guests were encouraged to drink as much as they want to and falling asleep and 'horseplay' was acceptable. In these terms, while the home is perhaps the central location for middle-class drinking practices there is an understood set of rules and rituals where drunken behaviour is accepted as long as it occurred in appropriate setting. Nonetheless, Hunt (1991, 419) is clear in his assessment that the idea that middle class drinking behaviour as a norm that should be aspired to by the 'un-civilized' working class fails to take into account the range of acceptable middle class drinking behaviour and that 'much of the behaviour, if transferred to a different social setting and performed by a different social groups, would be defined as unacceptable and problematic.'

Writers have also noted important issues concerning marginalization and alienation bound up with alcohol consumption in rural areas. For example, Kelly and Kowalyszyn (2003) discuss the association of alcohol and family problems in remote indigenous Australian communities. The research speaks against a wide held perception about aboriginal drinking cultures and show that the large proportion of Aboriginal Australians do not drink to excess. However, for the small proportion of people who have severe alcohol problems, family structures, values and obligations of Aboriginal families ensures that associations of family/

alcohol problems are encountered and experienced in specific ways. As such, Kelly and Kowalyszyn (2003) show how the combination of the limitations of alcohol support services in rural areas and family contexts where aggression and alcohol combine, family cohesion means that problems are often not disclosed. However, conversely they suggest that family cohesion is nonetheless a useful resource in attempting to tackle alcohol related aggression.

In a similar vein, Philo et al. (2002) look at the relationship between alcohol and mental health in respect to rural areas in Scotland. Their research investigates both the important symbolic contribution of drinking to regional identity, but also how excessive drinking and drunkenness are an accepted and important element of local social relations. Elaborating on this position, Philo et al. show how alcohol is bound up with emotional geographies around a number of issues. These include hospitality, a lack of leisure opportunities, relaxation and drinking as a reward, coping strategies and both isolation and belonging. They highlight the ways in which these geographies are gendered, with men's heavy drinking tending to take place in public whilst women's heavy drinking is more private and solitary and thus a constitutive element of exclusionary social relations.

In this section we have highlighted the way in which the relationship between alcohol consumption and rurality has been conceptualized. We have described the rich variety of work focused on a fascinating range of topics in diverse rural locations around the world. Such progress notwithstanding, there has nonetheless been a tendency for this work to be limited due to the problems with case study based research outlined in the Introduction. In the remainder of this chapter we look in detail at one issue – young people and alcohol consumption – in order to show how unpacking the similarities, differences, connectivities and mobilities between and within rural spaces and places (and in comparison to urban drinking practices) offers the opportunity for more sophisticated theoretical perspectives on drinking in the countryside to be developed.

Alcohol and Young People in the Countryside

As noted in the previous chapter, young people; drunk, violent and out of control in cities has been central to political, policy and popular debates. In contrast, in rural areas the 'moral components' (Kraack and Kenway 2002, 146) of country life alludes to the way that rural communities are viewed as close-knit, harmonious environments. In the countryside adults, children and young people thus live out a simple/pure existence free from the stress, dangers and corruptions of urban life (Ward 1990). This simple dichotomy has been increasingly troubled, however, by writers who highlight the flows of people, information and influences between urban and rural environments (Lash and Urry 1994). For example, Yarwood (2001, 2005) suggests that notions of the 'country idyll' are often constructed and sustained by influential 'in-coming' groups within the rural community, who act to protect their lifestyle and in doing so seek to exclude those who are perceived as threatening to traditional way of life. Yarwood identifies the inward migration of middle-class retirees and second home buyers who are keen to fulfil their fantasy of escaping the city to live in rural isolation as being central to this process. Taking this argument further Glendinning (2003) notes that young people in the countryside now experience similar problems of criminalization and surveillance in public spaces as urban youth. However, in making this point Glendinning challenges understandings of idyllic country living by pointing out that isolation and a lack of a public 'voice' compound these problems ensuring that young people living in rural areas are in fact more vulnerable to exclusion than young people in cities.

For example, Kraack and Kenway (2002, 148) consider Paradise, a small tourist town in New South Wales, Australia where young men are stigmatized in a number of different ways. Public space in Paradise is described as 'a theatre of masculinity', where swaggering overconfidence, rudeness, drink and drugs parties, and young people hanging around pubs are shown to be representative of depictions of young people. Beach parties, noise and mess, vomit, broken glasses – young people lying in the gutter or described as stoned 'zombies' are some of the images associated with young people. Kraack and Kenway (2002) argue that such representations are deeply entwined within dynamic globalizing processes that impact on community and individual identity. Along with broader structural changes where Paradise has changed from a traditional 'hard working, hard drinking' whaling shanty town to being dominated by tourist and retiree cultures, new residents have been campaigning for strict controls or banning of beach parties (near where most of the retirees have their houses on the beach front). In response, young people especially 'boys' have responded to the anti-young feel of the town and being cast as personification of the anti-idyll by exaggerating and aggravating the intergenerational tension. In rural south Wales, Jones (2002) also notes how deviant and disorderly behaviour has become a marker of cultural identity and that in migration is fuelling conflict between incomers and local young people. Yarwood (2001) offers a way to conceptualize such geographies of alcohol, drinking and drunkenness by highlighting the need to unpack how such discourses are bound up with geographies of crime, where fear of crime is underpinned in terms of views of what is a cultural threat to cherished ways of life that are considered to be 'under attack'.

In such rural areas, Shucksmith et al. (1997) suggests the need to highlight the ways in which children and young people are being stigmatized, misunderstood, and where their needs become invisible and/or unmet. For example, in Eden, national concerns over young people 'binge drinking' in public spaces has ensured that strategies and policies that replicate those undertaken in urban areas are now being translated to the countryside. The introduction of Closed Circuit Television (CCTV) in towns and villages, for instance, can be seen to be a direct response to concerns that young people's drunken behaviour was increasing and that rural life is being undermined by the opening of commercial venues that did not fit with images of the countryside pub. Indeed, interviews with key stakeholders from rural agencies and service providers highlight that the issue of young people binge drinking (and in particular young women's behaviour and safety) had become a key local issue (see Leyshon 2006; Tucker and Matthews 2001; and Chapter 4 this volume). It was also acknowledged, however, that constructions of binge drinking in national media, rather than as a response to a significant problem unfolding in Eden was the most important influence in prompted the introduction of CCTV. This local response in the context of national debate is best explained by Yarwood (2001) who highlights how restructuring in the countryside has led to heightened levels of anxiety, often expressed as fear of crime and that 'urban problems' are presented as eroding rural ways of life.

The historic strength of temperance organizations in Eden is also important in understanding the nature of anti-young people/anti-alcohol discourses. In pre-industrial rural societies, 'the pub' was one of the few social spaces open to rural residents; however, the growth of Christianity alongside political and economic change ensured that these venues became the exclusive domain of men (Dean 2002). While Eden has long history of hard drinking by working-class men as a traditional part of agricultural life the strength of Methodism in the area ensured the development of an active temperance movement in the nineteenth century. One of the most prominent groups was the Band of Hope which remained active in the area until the late twentieth century, albeit with declining influence after the Second World War ensuring that many local residents still recount tales of annual marches and playing in sports matches organized by temperance groups. As such, the echoes of traditional male working-class rural drinking culture continue to have an impact on the consumption landscape in contemporary Eden. While Penrith, the largest town, has witnessed a growth of more diverse 'sophisticated' and 'urban' drinking venues targeting the middle-classes, women and young people, there remains a dominance of traditional, male working-class pubs. Despite this the town is a magnet for younger drinkers who, despite often having to travel to considerable distances to get to Penrith in an area with very limited transport.

In contrast to policy and popular concerns focused on young people and drinking in public space respondents also highlighted that apparent acceptability of underage drinking. However, it was also suggested that the close-knit nature of social relations in rural communities acts as a deterrent to young people drinking to excess and behaving in anti-social ways. Indeed respondents of all ages and social groups suggested that most licensees or managers are likely to have known the underage young people that they are serving since childhood (and their families) ensuing social control in both commercial venues and other informal public drinking spaces. It is in this context that some rural commercial venues provide socially sanctioned underage access to alcohol:

> The majority of people … who we've found have consumed alcohol who were trying to get into the junior disco are female. And it's Mum's and Dad's who've given the females the drink, you know, little Suzie's had a bottle of Lambrusco before she's gone out and then she's gone to little Sarah's parents who've given them a couple of bottles of whatever, alcopops, you know and they turn up and

we've got this and then you sit down with parents and they say 'well what's wrong with having a drink before they go out?'

(Superintendent Cumbria Police)

Such depictions of parents' liberal attitude towards young people's drinking can be read both as a response to the limitations of rural living and a product of the changing nature of intergenerational relations (See Chapter 6). Alcohol consumed in the pub or at home, is considered as an important part in the social lives of rural adults because of the lack of other night-time economy activities in the countryside. In this acknowledgement most parents in our research recognized that the opportunities for young people's social lives are equally constrained, and they thus often (if sometimes reluctantly) supported their child's drinking activities in order to compensate for their rural isolation.

Indeed, it is well established in the rural geography literature that there are few places for older teenagers to go for youth entertainment (Matthews et al. 2000). Whereas urban young people have the option of cinemas, bowling alleys, late-night shopping venues and so on (though some young people were priced out or driven out by over zealous security guards) such opportunities do not often exist in rural areas. As such, young people growing up in the countryside are restricted by the limitations of rural public transport services and thus depend on friends or parents to chauffer them around (David and Ridge 1997). Young people in the countryside thus have less opportunity to hang out in commercial venues and other visible public spaces and to develop their own identities away from the gaze of their parents than their urban counterparts (Matthews et al. 2000).

It is not surprising then that most young people described their first experiences of drinking as taking place within family contexts. In these instances, young people consider that their drinking was supported by their families in order to encourage them to stay in the safe space of the home (see Chapter 3) or to provide them with a safe space to meet before going out together to commercial venues. Other research has also identified an implicit tolerance of underage drinking in rural communities. For example, Leyshon (2005, 2008) shows how young men often 'got into' pubs when they were underage by going with their parents (usually fathers) and used their knowledge of village biographies to ingratiate themselves with 'the locals' or by finding work in pubs. Respondents also argued that young people exercise more self-governance in the countryside than in urban areas and that limited anonymity tended to discourage the worst excesses of anti-social behaviour because young people are all too aware that drunken rowdiness is likely to be witnessed by friends, family and potential future employers:

[For young people] ... it's sort of yeah, it's not maybe so much they know my Mum but as opposed to they speak to your employer or whatever ... You don't want to make such a fool of yourself in a very small place because people do get disapproving and you know, you might need the opportunity.

(Anne Moyles, Eden, 35–44, Female, NS-SEC 3)

It is clear that in contrast to national debate, local policy responses and local media depictions of public concern, many respondents acknowledged that young peoples drinking practices were specifically related to the distinct characteristics of rural cultural life.

Leyshon (2005; 2008) also reflects on the complex social rules that circulate around alcohol in rural areas, in particular degree of drunkenness and type of behaviour that was considered acceptable within peer groups. In our rural case study area, both men and women expressed a desire to control their drinking (for example adjusting what they drink or pacing their levels of drinking) in order to avoid becoming the subject of ridicule among their peers although with distinctly different reasons. Women expressed concerns about appearing to be sexually promiscuous, whilst young men were concerned with seeming weak or childish for not being able to 'hold their drink'. For example, Lisa Turner (18–25) explains that whereas she stops drinking at the point she feels ill or feels she is making a 'show of herself' her male friends do not exhibit the same level of control:

> They [young men] just sort of carry on going just for the sake of, you know even if they see, like girls will admit when they're feeling ill won't they? Whereas lads are more likely to carry on drinking and expect it to … my boyfriend used to like drink quite a lot and then whenever he went outside he'd always be sick and then he'd just carry on drinking the rest of the night but I just really couldn't do that … If I got to that stage I'd just go home
>
> (Lisa Turner, Eden, 18–25, Female, NS-SEC 2)

However, their assessment of men's behaviour was not shared by all our male research participants. For example, Reese Holt (18–25) sought to control his drinking partly due to a practical concern about getting home and the response of his parents with whom he lives:

> I've never been paralytic sort of thing. I've been quite drunk but I haven't been that bad. I just stop myself. I don't want to go that far. Well you don't want to make a prat out of yourself and you don't want to be left in a ditch. [laughs]. My parents would probably absolutely destroy me if I did it so.
>
> (Reece Holt, Eden, 18–25, Male, NS-SEC 2)

Indeed, the issue of getting home was an important control on young people's drinking as unlike urban youngsters with access to night buses and black cabs, the only taxis that will take these young people to outlying villages are those which are pre-booked in advance.

The informal drinking spaces created by young people in the countryside also offer important insights into geographies of alcohol, drinking and drunkenness. While using informal space, for example meeting at friends house to begin drinking before going out, are practices also seen in urban areas, drinking in informal public spaces in this rural area is not, unlike in urban area, only the realm of illicit underage drinkers but also young adults in small towns and villages who have negligible access to commercial premises after the pubs close. Parks, scenic view shelters and cemeteries are examples of where underage drinkers and other young people aged eighteen to twenty five meet to drink in locations remote from residential properties and the eye of anyone other than late-night dog walkers. In these terms, where small groups of young people are involved in late-night alcohol consumption in public spaces then their rowdy or disorderly behaviour (associated with urban 'binge drinking') often remains 'hidden'. This relative lack of visibility helps explain why moral panics about binge drinking are less evident amongst rural residents.

Such practices help to explain how the most common response amongst interviewees of diverse ages was that public disorder stemming from binge drinking was an urban not a rural phenomenon. Unlike some local policy makers who were keen to identify young people drunk, violent and out of control as a burgeoning issue in Eden, most residents thought that the issue was one they were aware of from the press but was not one they were personally likely to encounter. However, their argument was not that people do not drink to excess – and some were even happy to admit that there was sometimes violence and disorder – but overall, that there was simply not a fear of alcohol-related disorder as disturbance:

> I don't worry about it [binge drinking] because I suppose where I live it's, it doesn't at all affect me [edit] but I can see in an urban environment that that would be quite threatening if you're, you know wanting to walk just because the others are drunk and there are lots of them, if you're actually you know at pub turning out time wanting to walk through a city, having been to the theatre or something like that, then I think, I can see why it concerns people [edit]. It's not something I get particularly over excited about, it has to be said, but then it's quite easy to not, as I say if I'm cocooned in a little village somewhere and it's nothing, I don't experience it, you know, so that's, it's something I'm reading in the newspaper and it isn't something I've experienced at all.
>
> (Audrey Bennett, Eden, 45–54, Female, NS-SEC 1)

> I think it is a city problem. It's not a problem we have. I mean there is, there is anti-social behaviour round here and there's, you know people that binge drink and that but it's [edit] you don't have much of a problem with it, because there's not a, a concentration of people …
>
> (Anne Moyles, Eden, 35–44, Female, NS-SEC 3)

Adults thus saw drinking amongst young people as an entirely normal process, as a phase through which young people pass:

> Not all of them do it, but a few seem to go over the top a bit but it's, it's like anything else, especially if you're in your teens you tend to overdo everything virtually … They just, teenagers are a bit daft category I think.
>
> (Colin Bellis, Eden, 65+, Male, NS-SEC 3)

Well I've been going out like 12 years, and I think it's always been the same. Maybe there is more emphasis put on it now but even when I started going out, there was people binge drinking then so [edit] I think they suddenly woke up and realized that there could be a problem.

(Helen Winner, Eden, 24–34, Female, NS-SEC 5)

I don't think people drink any more than they used to. I just think that it's just that the media has picked up on it.

(Julie Dodd, Eden, 35–44, Female, NS-SEC 6)

Indeed to a large degree most middle-aged residents were happy to admit that drinking to excess was something they had done themselves when young, and even that young people today were more sensible than they had been in the ways in which they managed their drinking.

While such relaxed attitude to young people's alcohol consumption is illuminating, such findings also need to be seen in the context of the normality of alcohol consumption in rural areas. Indeed, research on parenting suggests that the nature of intergenerational relations is changing. Traditionally parents have had 'natural' authority over children sustained through laws and everyday norms about the appropriate behaviour of adults and children (Jamieson and Toynbee 1989). However, it is now suggested that parents have sought closer, less hierarchical relationships with their children with the consequence that some of their 'natural' authority has been eroded (Ambert 1994; Wyness 1997). Rather than laying down the law with their children parents are more willing to invite discussion and to negotiate their relationships and rather, than children having a responsibility to be dutiful sons and daughters, the onus is on parents to maximize their children's potential by providing them with an idyllic childhood (in mainly material ways) and all opportunities that they themselves were denied. Thus, it becomes parents responsibility in rural areas to encourage sensible drinking rather than total avoidance of alcohol reflecting both a reluctance to assert a hierarchical – 'do as I say but not as I do' – relationship, and a desire to ensure that their children enjoy growing up in the countryside (see Chapter 6).

Conclusion

In this chapter we have presented research that has considered the relationships between alcohol consumption and class, gender, age and recent restructuring of rural life. It can be argued that while offering rich and detailed studies from diverse locations throughout the world, research on rural alcohol consumption has tended to be dominated by a case-study approach which focuses on specific locations and particular topics. Taking a contrasting approach here, considering the growing recognition of the flows of people, information and influences between urban and rural environments (Lash and Urry 1994) as our starting point, we have examined how particular urban-centred discourse play out in Eden, Cumbria. The analysis has shown that policy discourse does transfer to rural areas from cities. Depending on your standpoint, the consequences of such policy transfer has either been to nip trouble in the bud in rural areas before it gets out of hand, or alternatively to expose rural young people to greater levels of surveillance and control, for lesser behaviour, than their urban counterparts (Yarwood 2002, 2005). Nonetheless it is clear that concern about binge drinking has also been transformed by rural policy makers in a way that makes it more appropriate for their isolated communities, most notably through their emphasis on underage drinking.

Rather than simply problematizing 'binge drinking' though such public and policy discourses, our purpose in this chapter has also been to explore young people's alcohol consumption, and older residents reactions to it, as a socio-cultural process in a particular time-spaces. This strategy has been important as it emphasizes the normality, the taken-for-grantedness, of young people's drinking in rural communities. Notwithstanding some local policy initiatives designed to reduce limited night-time disturbance most older residents regard 'binge drinking' as a city problem which they are aware of via through the media but which had no immediate impact on their own lives. Picking up on the construction of 'binge drinking' in the wider media, these residents imagine 'binge drinking' not in terms of volume of alcohol consumed, but more significantly in terms of urban late-night alcohol-fuelled public disorder, which was not something they witnessed to any significant extent in their own locality. By contrast, the often large amounts of alcohol consumed by rural young people were rarely regarded as problematic.

This difference between the ways that young people's behaviour is read by residents in a rural, as compared to urban, environment is also a product of the distinct characteristics of rural cultural life as well as changes in intergenerational relations (see Chapter 6). In terms of rural life, alcohol plays a significant part in local culture. The pub has traditionally played an important role in village communities as a social space, especially for men. Despite broader socio-economic changes in rural communities the lack of entertainment and leisure spaces in the countryside mean that the pub, as well as increasing home-based alcohol consumption, provide the focus for many adults' social lives. As such, young people's drinking – in pubs and in informal spaces – is not only tolerated but in many cases regarded as normal behaviour by adults aware that their children (like themselves) have limited other social opportunities (Matthews et al. 2000). Respondents also pointed to the close-knit nature of social relations in this rural community in ensuring that there is little trouble. Greater informal social surveillance than found in urban areas and the fact that young people exercise more self-governance, aware as they are that there is less anonymity in the countryside than in urban areas were also highlighted to be key characteristics of rural drinking practices. Moreover, the inevitability of young people's exposure to alcohol, along with changes which mean parents are more likely to see their role as facilitators of young people's enjoyment of their youth rather than controllers of it (Jamieson and Toynbee 1989; Wyness 1977; Valentine 2004), means that a liberal consensus comes to dominate amongst parents who construct their role as introducing young people to sensible – that is socially sanctioned – drinking practices.

What is most striking about the accounts of young people is their congruence with the views of older residents. Rather than describing a youth culture distinctly apart from the lives of older residents in the area, young people's descriptions of their lifestyles mirror those of their post-war parents and their views are often in line with a wide variety of older residents. Thus young people, like older generations, construct binge drinking as a city problem centred on the risks of alcohol-related anti-social behaviour, behaviour from which they too feel safe in this rural area (at the same time as they describe the complex social relations surrounding young people's landscapes of drinking in rural areas). As Glendinning (2003) points out, young people themselves express feelings of safety in their rural homes, at the same time as comparing it to cities which they tend to view as less safe. This identification with their environment which gives young people a distinct and strong sense of place has a significant impact upon their experiences and understandings of alcohol within local culture. Indeed, running through the accounts of younger and older residents alike is a sense of safety around rural drinking. Low crime rates; (a notion) of few drugs; a tendency not to have large concentrations of drunken people in public spaces and the security given by knowing other local people when out at night all mean that parents and young people allow themselves to be complacent about rural drinking.

Overall, the picture which emerges from this study is one of partial linkages, but also discursive boundary maintenance between urban and rural areas. For while policy makers are happy to take on an urban-centred 'binge drinking' agenda in their rural area, this moral panic is largely rejected by older and younger local residents alike. While this may be a rare instance where older residents reject a moral panic about youth culture, and the imposition of a surveillant urban agenda onto rural communities, the problem with this consensus, however, is that running though the discussions of local residents of all ages is a lack of awareness of the health risks of heavy or long-term drinking. This lack of appreciation of the health consequences of drinking is, as we identified earlier, of concern to local policy professionals with regard to underage drinking, and as our own research showed affects considerable numbers of people of all ages in the area. Ultimately, the consequence of public and policy discussion which constructs 'binge drinking' as problematic in the context or urban, alcohol-fuelled disorder is to mask other – in this case health – problems associated with alcohol consumption in a broader diversity of locales. The evidence in this chapter suggests that work to prevent and address alcohol misuse amongst young people needs to not only address urban drinking but also to acknowledge and find ways of responding to the importance of alcohol in rural communities. In particular, young people's drinking needs to be understood and addressed in relation to their parents' attitudes to and use of alcohol, and the nature of intergenerational relations within rural households and communities. At the same time the research highlights the need for rural researchers to pay attention to the specific consumption patterns that develop in the context of rural lifestyles.

In this chapter we have sough to advance research focused on rural alcohol consumption by focusing on the similarities, differences, connectivities and mobilities between urban and rural areas as well as within different spaces. In doing so we have considered how specific ideological dimensions of the urban/rural underpin geographies of alcohol consumption and attitudes towards drunkenness. In the next chapter we develop this argument further by turning our attention to alcohol consumption at home.

Chapter 3
Home

This chapter takes the prevalent, but apparently unremarkable, nature of domestic drinking as its starting point. It refers first to the academic and policy literature in order to explore why the UK's most prevalent drinking environment has attracted so little attention. We then use quantitative and qualitative data from our questionnaire survey and in-depth interviews to explore the nature and meaning of home drinking for our study participants. In doing so, we build on the argument made in the previous chapters in order to show how public and private drinking environments are inextricably linked, and explore what alcohol means to people as they move into and out of the home. We conclude by emphasizing that ideologies of home underpin domestic drinking practices, and serve to insulate those drinking to harmful or hazardous levels from concern (see Holloway et al. 2008).

Missing Home: Envisioning a Cartography of Drinking in the UK

As human geographers increasingly engage with key issues around alcohol and drunkenness we need to pick up on some of the best practice seen in alcohol studies and avoid the limitations noted in the introductory chapter (see Jayne et al. 2008a). One key issue is that we need to think about the ways in which alcohol is conceptualized in public and academic debate as this ultimately frames the issues of concern in different ways. Kneale and French's (2008) historical and contemporary analysis of the geographical imaginaries associated with changing conceptions of problem drinking provides us with an insightful route into these issues. They trace the ways in which alcohol has been framed as a social problem in three different time periods. In the first of these which they label as Temperance (up to the 1950s) alcoholism was regarded as a problem either because of an individual's lack of moral fibre and/or the circumstances in which they lived (e.g. deprived urban neighbourhoods), suggesting intervention to remove/resist temptation and alleviate poverty. Between the 1950s and the 1970s alcoholism was medicalized, coming to be seen as a biological rather than a moral disease and thus in need of medical treatment. From the 1970s, however, this medical model was challenged by a new form of epidemiology which posited drinking as an issue for the whole population not simply alcoholics, and this has resulted in public health policies – such as unit-based safe drinking guidelines recommending limits to daily and weekly consumption.

These different conceptualizations of alcohol as a problem not only led to different policy interventions, they also underpin differing geographical imaginaries of problem drinking (Kneale and French 2008). For social reformers such as Joseph Rowntree, Arthur Sherwell and Charles Booth who were concerned with the supply of drink and poor social conditions this lead to an imperative to map public houses and locate clusters of problem drinking. By contrast, 'the spatial imagination of disease theory tended to concern spaces of diagnosis and treatment – specialist hospital units, doctors' surgeries, self-help groups' (Kneale and French 2008, 15), and while social and supply causes were not ignored, the cluster argument became less important as pubs etc were only seen as a danger to individual problem drinkers not the population as a whole. However, the return to 'social' view of alcohol which is seen in the epidemiological/public health approach has brought the cluster approach, with its desire to map the supply and consequences of alcohol, back into focus. This has involved mapping at a variety of scales but, and as Kneale and French (2008, 15) put it, '[t]he main geographical expression of the problem is the city centre cluster'.

Kneale and French's (2008) analysis is thus extremely useful in demonstrating how particular conceptions of 'problem' drinking result in an emphasis on city centre clusters in the contemporary period. Like many geographical imaginaries, this vision is a highly partial one and is as much of interest for what it excludes and that which it includes. Indeed, it is interesting to note that while most political and media attention has been focused on city centre drinking in recent years, drinking at home is a relatively neglected but highly significant part of the market. In the UK 46 per cent of drinking adults do most of their drinking at home (compared with 42 per cent in Germany, 31 per cent in France and 23 per cent in Spain – Mintel 2003). Table 3.1 demonstrates the popularity of home drinking: in 2004 48 per cent of UK adults had a drink at home at least once a week, compared with only 28 per cent who do so outside the home (Mintel 2005). In this context, the off-trade in the UK accounts for 35 per cent of value sales (a figure which underplays volume as profits per unit are lower in the off- than the on-trade, a fact intensified in recent years by deep discounting in supermarkets – Mintel 2007a). Moreover, the market has shown significant growth in recent years: in real terms the off-trade saw a 16 per cent growth in sales between 2002 and 2006, while the figure for the on-trade was only 1 per cent (Mintel 2007a).

Despite the economic importance of home drinking, and its popularity as a social practice, the relative silence about home drinking in public debate is reproduced in academia where comparatively little has been written about it within the geographical and wider social science literature. The Office for National Statistics (ONS) provides some very useful large-scale survey evidence about domestic drinking levels, including its variation by social group (Lader 2009), though the nature of their data means they are unable to explore the social practices which result in these trends (and not all of their surveys of alcohol consumption take drinking location into account (Goddard 2008; Rickards et al. 2004). Studies at the sub-national scale which focus on processes rather than statistical trends tend to take one of two forms, both of which are valuable. On the one hand there are studies which consider the problems associated with drinking, for example domestic

Table 3.1   UK Adults' Frequency of Drinking Alcoholic Beverages in and out of Home, 2004 (%)

	Out-of-Home	In-Home
All users	67.5	75.4
Once a day	1.6	12.5
2 or 3 times a week	11.8	22.3
Once a week	14.5	13.2
2 or 3 times a month	12.9	9.9
Once a month	9.2	5.2
Less than once a month	17.5	12.3
Non-users	32.5	24.6

Source: Adapted from Mintel (2005), Figure 1, no page number

violence (Galvani 2006; Hutchinson 1999; Klostermann and Fals-Stewart 2006), or the management of socially marginal forms of drinking, for example drinking amongst older people who are recipients of home care/care home support (Herring and Thom 1997; Brennan and Greenbaum 2005). On the other hand, researchers have considered the importance of parental influence and home environment in shaping young people's drinking practices (Komro et al. 2007; Lowe et al. 1993). Noticeable for their absence are in-depth studies which examine the everyday home drinking practices of a broader diversity of social groups who would not necessarily consider themselves as having an alcohol problem, or to be suffering the consequences of other people's problematic drinking.

This is an exciting time for alcohol policy and research; however, recent developments seem to point to potential changes in the geographical imaginary of problem drinking. In policy terms, Government concern has been 'to move on from the battle to clear the streets of binge-drinking youths and tackle the drinking culture hidden behind the sitting room curtains' (Boseley 2007, 12: see also BBC News 2007; HM Government 2007; Smith and Womack 2007). From an academic perspective, Kneale and French (2008, 246) argue that we need to move beyond the city centre, and reason that '[i]f we change the way we frame the problem, and consider the persistent appeal of the disease model, then other actors and sites become visible', including medicine, self-help (such as Alcoholics Anonymous), doctors surgeries, insurance offices, and suburban homes.

Following their lead and reconsidering the disease model, which was common in thinking on alcohol between the 1950s and 1970s, would open up some profitable lines of research. In relation to the home, however, we argue that it would be more beneficial to move beyond approaches which routinely conceptualize drinking in pathological terms, and to consider drinking as a broad-ranging social practice, rather than as a necessarily problematic behaviour. This difference in the way alcohol is framed matters as it shapes precisely which homes might be opened up for study – those of people already labelled as problem drinkers through the disease model, or a wider variety of homes. This wider variety of homes is important, we argue, both for an analysis of the importance of drinking in wider culture (see also Social Issues Research Centre (SIRC) 1998), but also as it allows us insights into who does, and does not, become labelled/label themselves as problem drinkers. Such an analysis, which explores the everyday drinking practices of a diversity of social groups, is a key concern for this chapter. In the following section we now go on to use our questionnaire and interview data to explore the nature and meaning of domestic alcohol consumption in the UK.

Domestic Drinking Practices, Social Meanings and Social Difference

The contemporary geographical imaginary of drinking as a city centre issue contrasts starkly with our survey results which show that for this representative cross-section of people in Eden and Stoke-on-Trent the most common venue for drinking is the home. Indeed, as Table 3.2 shows, the popularity of drinking in one's own home is most closely followed by the popularity of drinking in friends' and family's houses. Fewer people report regularly drinking in pubs/bars, restaurants, hotels, clubs and public events, although pubs/bars and restaurants were significantly more popular in urban Stoke-on-Trent-on-Trent than rural Eden. This evidence, which resonates with Government statistics (Lader 2009) and market research highlighting the growing significance of the off-trade (Mintel 2007), emphasizes the pressing need to explore the geographies of domestic drinking.

Drinking at home can be an important part of home-based sociability, and 56 per cent of people report being likely to drink when having a night in. The widespread nature of this practice means that people likely to have a drink on a night in were found in diverse social groups. It is notable that the popularity of drinking on a night in the house did not vary by gender, although there was some variation by age (young people were split on the issue; middle-aged groups

Table 3.2   Regular Drinking Venues in the Past 12 months (%)

	Total	Eden	Stoke-on-Trent
Home	72.9	72.5	73.3
Friends'/family's houses	63.4	63.8	63.0
Pubs/bars	59.6	55.2	64.4
Restaurants	52.7	48.8	57.4
Hotels	28.2	26.2	30.4
Clubs	22.7	20.3	25.3
Public events	21.1	19.2	23.2

Source: Questionnaire survey

Note: The term 'regular' was self-defined by respondents

were more likely to drink on a night in; over 65s were more likely to avoid this), social class (most notably there were fewer abstainers amongst professional and managerial respondents, and more amongst small employers and own account workers), and religion (those with no religion were less likely to abstain – see also Lader 2009).

Notwithstanding the general nature of this picture, in which home drinking emerges as a very popular activity involving people from many different walks of life, a significant minority of our sample did not drink at home. This was not a homogeneous group, and their reasons for avoiding alcohol in the home were linked to their religious affiliations, health problems, as well as social factors around taste and preferred drinking locations. For example, Bazid, who we discuss in Chapters 4 and 5, avoided drinking at home because of religious prohibitions on drink in his particular belief community. Others have serious health problems. Julie (Eden, 35–44, NS-SEC 6) is an alcoholic who having been dry for three years will not have alcohol in the house. Jeremy Collins, by contrast, has a severe medical condition which means that, while his wife can drink at home, he is now T-Total for health reasons (Stoke-on-Trent, Male, 59, NS-SEC 1). For a third group it was more simple, as people such as Linda (Stoke-on-Trent, Female, 45–54, NS-SEC 1), simply didn't like the taste of alcohol and it consequentially played only a small role in her life. Finally, there was another group, usually male, who enjoyed drinking but deemed it a social activity and, like Rob in the previous chapter, therefore only drank out of the house in the company of others:

Interviewer: What are the best things about drinking then …?

Sam: It's probably the social aspect of it really. It's probably why I don't drink in the house really; I don't drink on my own.
(Sam Boyer Stoke-on-Trent, 35–44, Male, NS-SEC 3)

Norman: I'm really either all or nothing. If I, if I go to the pub, I'll drink a lot, if I stay in the house I'll drink absolutely nothing.
(Norman Bath, Stoke-on-Trent, 35–44, Male, NS-SEC 4)

For the majority who do drink in the home, alcohol consumption takes a variety of forms. Dinner parties top the list of occasions on which people would drink in the domestic environment, with 36 per cent of people being likely to have dinner parties and drink at these events. Anthropological research suggests that drinking is – in most times and cultures – a social act which through reciprocity aids the establishment and maintenance of social bonds (SIRC 1998; see also Burns et al. 2002; Putnam 2000). In the context of UK-based home drinking, the sharing of alcohol and food with those from outside the family unit demonstrates that the home is not, as wider literature on the geographies of home also demonstrates (Tolia-Kelly 2004; Walsh 2006), simply the bounded private world of family members, rather in this case it is a place of sociability into which wider members of the community are drawn, and through which extra-familial friendships are maintained.

This practice is not, however, universal as the stereotypically middle-class image the term dinner party conjures up (see for example, Graff 2007) might lead us to suspect. Rather in our study it varies in a significant and linear fashion with class and age, being more popular amongst younger and more advantaged social groups. Nevertheless, this does not mean that such practices are solely confined to these groups, a fact which becomes even more evident when we take into consideration both formal and informal events:

> If you are at a dinner party and you've got something nice, a bottle of wine, the right bottle of wine with a meal, sort of, adds something.
>
> (Malcolm Patterson, Stoke-on-Trent, 55–64, Male, NS-SEC 1)

> [W]e had a dinner party last Saturday here and 6 bottles of wine went you know [between the 6] ... [he continues later] ... Well if you have a dinner party. I mean it's not just drinking, it's the occasion and people want to enjoy themselves. And it doesn't matter, I mean I suppose, I don't think you could enjoy yourself if we didn't have the wine because it does unwind you ...
>
> (Terry Clarke, Stoke-on-Trent, 55–64, Male, NS-SEC 10)

> I have friends round on a Thursday or I go to theirs, I do drink a full bottle of red wine to myself. It doesn't touch the sides really, it doesn't affect me in any way. [She continues later] A group of us, about six of us, so girl friends. We have a takeaway at either one of our houses, you know once a week, it's a regular thing.
>
> (Jenny Rush, Stoke-on-Trent, 35–44, Female, NS-SEC 4)

These quotations begin to hint at some of the multiple roles alcohol plays in the home. As Malcolm Patterson suggests, the availability of an appropriate form of this commodity is crucial in the negotiation of complex systems of sociality, hospitality and reciprocity. This is evident in the imperative felt to offer visitors an appropriate alcoholic beverage of their choice. Many of our interviewees not only keep alcohol in their home which suited their own tastes, they also maintained a range of drinks they thought it appropriate to be able to offer visitors. Class differences do matter here as some low-income interviewees stressed that they bought alcohol when about to consume it as they could not afford to do otherwise. However, the hospitality imperative is sufficiently strong that some non-drinkers also kept alcohol in their house:

> Max: There's usually some [alcohol] knocking about [the house]. People, you know other people, drink it and people bring it, you know if you went around for dinner, they bring wine or I'd buy wine for people when they come round for dinner and it's not a, you know, dry house.

Interviewer: And does that surprise ... your friends and family that you don't drink but then you'll keep alcohol in the house for them if they want any?

Max: I think it please them more than surprises them. They don't think that they come to my house and they go on the wagon for the night.

(Max Speer, Stoke-on-Trent, 25–34, Male, NS-SEC 5)

As SIRC (1998, 31) argue, 'every drink is loaded with symbolic meaning, every drink conveys a message'. In this instance, having appropriate drink available for visitors delivers a message of hospitality, a message that both welcomes the visitors and marks out the host as considerate, and with some drink choices, appropriately cultured (Pettigrew 2002).

This social home drinking, with people from outside the household, while important, is only one aspect of domestic drinking. The bodily effects of alcohol alluded to by Terry Clarke above – whereby the first drink for most people depresses the parts of the brain that are associated with inhibition, increasing talking and self-confidence and reducing social anxiety (Mental Health Foundation 2006) – are equally important for some in their everyday use of alcohol to unwind after work. For while 36 per cent of people reported home drinking with dinner parties, 32 per cent reported drinking with standard meals, 26 per cent whilst watching DVDs/videos; 24 per cent whilst watching sport and 20 per cent whilst watching other television. Audrey Bennett, for example, who drinks wine with her meal every night, explains that both she and her partner work long hours and often have further work to finish when they get home. When she has sorted this out, she likes to drink wine whilst cooking and eating to help her switch off:

Well I think I like to switch off, because I tend to get home and ... sort out anything I need, because quite often I've been in different meetings and, sort all that out and then I actually start to relax when I start doing the cooking. This is when I'll want a glass of wine and [I'm] quite happy drinking while I'm in the kitchen doing the cooking. And that's me winding down really.

(Audrey Bennett, Eden, 45–55, Female, NS-SEC 1)

While for Audrey drinking whilst cooking is a key part of this process, other interviewees were equally happy to combine alcohol with a take away, while watching television or simply resting:

If it's been a hard day at work and what not, and it's just, I've got an empty evening ahead of me, I'll get some food and some alcohol and just sit round and chill.

(Allan Cummins, Stoke-on-Trent, 25–34, Male, NS-SEC 5)

I'd rather sit in the house than go and sit in a smoky [pub]. I'd rather have a bottle of wine and watch telly. [She continues later] I find it relaxes me and my husband likes it. It relaxes him, he's got quite a stressful job. [She continues later] Well normally, when we sit down like tonight we probably sit down and my husband will go and play his guitar, he's got his guitar, so he'll go and play the guitar and I'll probably watch Coronation Street, he hates anything like that, so he's out of the way, and then we'll sit down together about nine o'clock and then, I'd say a bottle of wine will last us two and half hours between us and that's it, bedtime.

(Charlotte Heaton, Stoke-on-Trent, 45–54, Female, NS-SEC 2)

I'm involved in quite, in a business that's very physical and I often come home absolutely jiggered, so you sit down with a gin and tonic don't you? And you recover, then you make a meal, and then you eat that and then the night goes on and then you go to bed. I take a whisky with me and that's often how my day is.

(Doris Humphreys, Eden, 60+, Female, NS-SEC3)

These processes of using alcohol to relax and wash away the mental (and in some cases physical) stresses of work are everyday in the sense that interviewees, unlike their public health counterparts (Patterson et al. 2005), regarded them as unremarkable. For some they were also literally part of their daily routine, though for others home consumption of alcohol is more sporadic:

[W]e might go through a week where we have a glass of wine, we actually might finish the bottle, we might do that two or three times one week, and then hardly drink for a week, a fortnight.

(Mike Kirkland, Eden, 45–54, Male, NS-SEC 5)

These bodily feelings associated with alcohol consumption lead in some cases to it being used as both a treat and a treatment (see Chapter 7). Margaret Sellers' consumption of alcohol illustrates both these trends. On the one hand, she views alcohol as something of a luxury with which she can reward herself:

[W]hat I really like doing to be really decadent, [is to] just take a big glass to bed, to bed with me when I'm reading. You know if you sort of think there's nothing to watch on telly, I'll take a big glass of wine to bed and read, and it's lovely, it feels really decadent. And, and relaxing and lovely, so I like to do that as well. I suppose it is a bit of a luxury, I'm treating myself and being kind of to myself sort of thing.

(Margaret Seller, Eden, 45–55, Female, NS-SEC 4)

This treat though can also be used as a treatment to help relieve excessive stress or feelings of depression (Burns et al. 2002):

I think I comfort drink if I have a bad day, or it's a Tuesday and I think, and there's not a bottle open, I think "oh sod it, that's what it's there for, I'll just have a glass of wine". But I wouldn't drink the whole bottle. [She continues later] …

I came home on Friday feeling really, really, really down, fed up and I opened
a bottle of cava, and I had the whole bottle with orange juice and I went to bed
at half past eight. I woke up feeling fantastic the next morning, so it obviously
did the trick …

(Margaret Sellers, Eden, 45–55, Female, NS-SEC 4)

This process is one the Mental Health Foundation (2006) refer to as self-medication,
and our findings support their stance that this is relevant in understanding why
many in the broader population drink and is not simply confined to those with
diagnosed mental health problems.

So far we have demonstrated that home is an open rather than permanently
bounded location (Massey 1995), being both a space of extra-familial sociality
and a site that for some requires protection from the invasion of work-based
stresses through domestic drinking. Home drinking as part of a night out is a subtly
different illustration of its links to other time-spaces and is an important part of a
night out for some, with 40 per cent likely to have a drink before they go out for a
night and 23 per cent likely to drink after coming home from a night out:

What I do now is I get a bottle of cider and I know that, I know that gets me
really drunk and so I just drink that and then that's it … [he continues later] …
I get drunk before I go out yeah….I just know it's is going to get me drunk so I
just have that and then that's it … I probably spend about, because we usually
play a drinking game, and probably only about an hour and a half and then go
out, just do a few bars, not really, I don't really drink much in the bar.

(Justin Donald, Eden, 18–24, Male, NS-SEC 1)

The quantitative data shows that this propensity to drink before a night out did
not vary by gender, but did differ significantly with age, religion and social class.
Unsurprisingly perhaps, those in the younger age range were over represented
amongst those very likely to drink before a night out, those over 55 were over
represented amongst those very unlikely to do so. Similarly, the fact that 47 per
cent of religious people are very unlikely to before going out compared with only
32 per cent of their secular counterparts is not unexpected (Galen and Rogers
2004). The relationship with class is less intuitive however: in general terms, those
from a higher social class are overrepresented amongst those who drink before a
night out (although all social groups are represented to some extent). Thus while
the qualitative data does provide occasional evidence of high and low-income
young people drinking to the point of drunkenness before they go out in order
to save money, financial constraints (which have been shown more broadly to
shape consumption rates (Rickards 2004; Mintel 2004)) seem to limit people on
lower incomes participation in this form of home drinking. Indeed, Hughes et al.'s
(2008) recent study shows that those who do drink at home before a night out then
drink similar amounts when out as those who had not, meaning that those who
drank before going out simply ended up drinking more.

In discussing this form of home drinking, which is more popular with but not confined to the young, we want to be careful not to 'Other' it from types of domestic consumption such as wine with a nice meal. This is important as there are similarities in these practices, including the use of alcohol to wind down:

> Ann: [We m]eet about half one, two, open the wine, you know, why not, talk about the day, chill out. And then we'll start getting ready to go out and then the vodka comes out … sometimes if we're feeling cheeky we'll have a couple of little bottles of alcopops … drink as we're getting ready. And people come, people come to my house and meet us there, and we'll drink vodka all together and then we'll go out and then we'll drink when we get back as well.

> Interviewer: So you'd be chatting about what the night's going to be like or where you're going or what kind of stuff?

> Ann: Yeah, yeah what we did last week … we'll talk about work as well, as we unwind, we'll talk about work and what's happened there, because Lucy has got quite a stressful job as well and we sort of really offload on each other and get it all out. Then we're ready to go out.
> (Ann Peters, Stoke-on-Trent-on-Trent, 25–34, Female, NS-SEC 1)

Another commonality is that the role of financial affordability, seen in relation to pre night-out drinking, is also evident in other domestic drinking practices. The recent increase in domestic drinking (Mintel 2007) appears to be fuelled by the greater affordability of, and easier access to, alcohol. Marjory Miller explains, for example, that there was less home drinking in the past because people simply could not afford it:

> You didn't have the money and the last thing…you'd go and do is buy a bottle of sherry or anything, if the next day you'd got nothing to put on the table, is it. So you didn't, you just didn't do it really.
> (Marjory Miller, Eden, 65+, Female, NS-SEC 4)

Indeed, many middle-class respondents explained that drinking wine at home had changed from being a rare or weekly treat to something which they could now afford on a regular basis as their own incomes increased (and perhaps more importantly as the price of wine has fallen relative to average earnings – Mintel 2005). In addition to price concerns, some older respondents were clear that wine had become more socially accessible as it now no longer required specialist knowledge to purchase it:

> [W]hen I was young, well there weren't supermarkets, but I mean the, the wine shops were, I mean you were almost reluctant to go in there. I mean, you know, they weren't friendly places, if you like, and you didn't go in to, to be made a

fool of if you didn't know much about the wine. I mean it wasn't just like off the shelves at Tesco's or anything like that.

(Anthony Oram, Eden, 65+, Male, NS-SEC 1)

This freer availability of alcohol through supermarkets (Burnett 1999) has been important in facilitating home drinking and changing the drinking landscape. In the words of one interviewee:

Sainsbury's is my local.

(Allan Cummins, Stoke-on-Trent, 25–34, Male, NS-SEC 5)

Changes in individuals' lives are another important influence on home drinking. The life course, and particularly significant events such as marriage/ partnership and the arrival of children, often mark changes in people's drinking practices. The most notable impact of the 'family' phase of the lifecycle is a shift away from the importance of commercial drinking venues, where new partners can be met, towards domestic drinking environments (see Valentine et al. 2007 for more details). This shift towards domestic drinking with marriage/cohabitation, and in some cases childrearing, has the effect of limiting some people's alcohol consumption. For Reginald, this was in part financially driven:

We didn't drink so much when we had children, you find a big change when your first child comes. [He continues later] You suddenly don't have quite so much money and there's only one of you then working whereas previously you're two and you settle down really and your life becomes boring.

(Reginald Best, Eden, 55–65, Male, NS-SEC 1)

Some mothers were also explicit that their childrearing responsibilities meant that they consumed less alcohol than in their youth as they needed to be able to get up early in the morning with young children, and wanted to be in a condition where they could respond to problems if required. Lone parent Helen Winner, for example, explains that she drinks Lambrusco or Lambrini, which are low alcohol drinks, so that she would be able to look after her daughter and drive her to hospital (which is some considerable distance away in this rural area) if she needed to:

I think that a lot of it is that I don't drink too much when I'm home because what happens if? ... The rest of my family live [name of location some distance away], and I was the only one of my sisters that could drive, but it's not as if anything happens I could ring my sister up ... and say oh my God, Lauren's had an accident can you come up, I've been drinking.

(Helen Winner, Eden, 24–34, Female, NS-SEC 5)

However, this pattern of low domestic alcohol consumption when children are very young is not universal, and increasingly less common as children get older. Mark, for example, explains that childrearing responsibilities shifted the location of his drinking into the home environment, while for Anne Moyles the shift from public to private consumption practices resulted in an increase rather than a decrease in the units of alcohol consumed:

> We couldn't go out because she had kids, she couldn't get a babysitter so, like Friday night we didn't go out, we stopped in so we'd get the beer in for Friday nights.
>
> (Mark Simpson, Stoke-on-Trent, 35–44, Male, NS-SEC 5)

> I don't go out to nightclubs anymore, we stay very local now, I do a lot more drinking at home, you know. Me and Stephen will crack open a bottle of wine most evenings, we don't go out to the pub that much, and we drink more than what we did, overall, [laughs] than when I was going out nightclubbing. ... Because we do it over the week and yeah I'll still get blotto most weekends and things like that. Just, we just do it sort of quietly, ... not going out nightclubbing, that sort of thing.
>
> (Anne Moyles, Eden, 35–44, Female, NS-SEC 3)

These domestic drinking practices started, in the summer and autumn of 2007, to become the focus of public and policy attention because of their negative health consequences (BBC News 2007; Boseley 2007; Smith and Womack 2007). Such health concerns were important in limiting domestic alcohol consumption for only a very small minority of our interviewees. As we discussed earlier, these people tended to have something significant in their own lives – such as alcoholism or severe physical health problems – which realized fears around alcohol in a fairly direct way. In the absence of factors such as these, significant concerns about health and domestic drinking were very few and far between. Malcolm, for example, had drunk more than recommended guidelines in the week prior to interview but reasoned:

> I've always taken the position that the, you know that, you know a little bit of what you fancy of anything probably doesn't do you any harm.
>
> (Malcolm Patterson, Stoke-on-Trent, 55–64, Male, NS-SEC1)

A lack of concern about the health consequences of drinking is something which is seen in relation to both home-based and extra-domestic drinking environments. Sometimes this lack of concern can reflect ignorance of recommended drinking levels.

> It's completely slipped my mind now how much you are supposed to have.
>
> (Jenny Rush, Stoke-on-Trent, 35–44, Female, NS-SEC 4)

It was far more common, however, for interviewees to have some (albeit incomplete) knowledge about sensible drinking (Lader 2009), but not to make a link between this and their own social practices. Sometimes individuals are aware of these but choose not to abide by them as they seem so unrelated to their social practices. Verity Beech, for example, chooses not to keep to these as the recommendations are incompatible with her lifestyle and, thus, she judges the limits to be too low:

> I think they're too low, and it's not that you can, apparently there's a, you can't really save them up can you? You can't like save up the units and have them all in one go, that's not recommended either.
>
> (Verity Beech, Stoke-on-Trent, 18–24, Female, NS-SEC 3)

As Annie Peters, who also drinks to harmful levels, explains:

> I don't [have any health concerns], you should do shouldn't you, because you see it everywhere and you know like alcohol is like one of the biggest killers out of any drug that there is, but you just, you just don't.
>
> (Ann Peters, Stoke-on-Trent, 25–34, Female, NS-SEC 1)

This lack of connection between fairly well publicized drinking guidelines and individual practices requires examination in a diversity of contexts, but our focus here is on the home environment. How then do individuals articulate their divergence from these recommended guideline in the domestic context? One strategy was to rely on signals from ones own body rather than what were regarded as the moving goalposts of recommended alcohol intake. Particularly important here is the notion that, as individual drinking events do not induce illness in the drinker, they can not be inherently unhealthy (and it is noteworthy in this context that harmful consequences of drinking are not symptomatically apparent until well developed – HM Government, 2007). Amanda Pinder, for example, shares a bottle of wine or two with her husband over their evening meal five or six evenings a week. At some points in her interview she expressed concern that this might be 'too much' but works hard to convince herself that this is not the case as she is not physically ill after alcohol consumption:

> I do have concerns about drinking but I, I still think that my drinking is within manageable limits, and I never feel ill after I've drunk [she continues later] … today with anything, clean your teeth, whatever you eat, how much you drink, you know the goalposts keep moving all the time, and it's difficult to be sure that, but I don't think it's harmful, not the amount I drink.
>
> (Amanda Pinder, Stoke-on-Trent, 55–64, Female, NS-SEC 2)

A second strategy was to argue that drinking at home with a meal was a healthy part of a Mediterranean lifestyle. Here studies which suggest that modest alcohol consumption (1 to 2 units a day) can have health benefits for men over 40 and post-menopausal women (HM Government 2007) were mobilized as part of a position that constructed wine drinking as healthy. Some deploying these arguments were not themselves heavy drinkers:

> [I like] red more than white. I've heard that's good for you. That's brilliant, it absorbs your cholesterol and clears out the blood vessels and I prefer red than white.
>
> (Maurice Haige, Stoke-on-Trent, 55–64, Male, NS-SEC 1)

Others, however, who did drink to hazardous or harmful levels, also deployed this argument. Audrey Bennett, for example, explained that alcohol needs to be considered in the context of a wider lifestyle, suggesting that a Mediterranean diet although high in alcohol also contained oily fish and was therefore healthier than one containing too much saturated fat. She, therefore, chose not to be panicked by what she regards as health scares stating that:

> I mean, I'm reasonably fit, I do eat healthy food, and I don't think that I'm seriously damaging myself by drinking wine with a meal each evening.
>
> (Audrey Bennett, Eden, 45–55, Female, NS-SEC 1)

In this way, the limited health benefits of small amount of alcohol consumption for some demographic groups have been mobilized to justify domestic drinking practices where alcohol intake can exceed Government guidelines. The combined result of these strategies is that hazardous/harmful domestic drinking, unlike public binge drinking, remains a normal, unremarkable, unproblematic practice in the eyes of many, notwithstanding the health and other problems such practices can cause (HM Government 2007).

Conclusions

Kneale and French (2008) have argued persuasively that the different ways in which concern about alcohol has been framed over time underpin discrete geographical imaginaries of problem drinking and shape distinct policy interventions. In the contemporary period, the framing of problem drinking through an epidemiological model has led to a geographical focus on the city centre cluster and detracted attention from domestic drinking which account for 43 per cent of the drinks market in terms of volume (Mintel 2003). The consequence of this is that an important part of British culture has remained hidden from academic and policy view. This study of the domestic practices of a diverse section of the population demonstrates the popularity of home drinking in a context where, for many, alcohol has become both more affordable and more socially accessible. This drinking in the domestic context is combined with a wide diversity of activities and the bodily effects of alcohol (most notably relaxation) were enjoyed alone, with family and with friends. Common across these different forms of domestic alcohol consumption, however, was the fact that many regarded home drinking as a pleasurable activity which smoothes their passage through everyday life.

In this chapter we have sought to avoid constructing the homes in which people drink as bounded, and instead drawn out the implications of wider connections for domestic alcohol consumption. These linkages from the positive webs of extra-familial social bonds which are formed and maintained as alcohol is involved in acts of hospitality and reciprocity, to the potential invasion of the home by stress associated with paid work (and some people's use of alcohol to rebound the home and make it impervious to this), to the links between changing landscapes of retailing, most notably the sale of alcohol through supermarkets, and the growing social and financial ease with which many can drink in the home. As we have seen through the course of the chapter these linkages can work in different ways for different groups, with social difference around age, religion and social class mattering most in statistical terms.

This focus on a broad diversity of drinkers stemmed from our rejection of the automatic problematization of alcohol. This does not lead us to suggest, however, that domestic drinking is never problematic for individuals or those around them – clearly it is (HM Government 2007; Hutchinson 1999; Brennan and Greenbaum 2005). Rather, we argue that by focusing on the broader population we enhance our understanding of wider drinking culture and in the process also deepen our understanding of problem drinking. At one level, focusing on the broader population serves to make the home more visible as it begins to moves us away from the dominant city-centre geographical imaginary of problem drinking in the 2000s. Refocusing on the home, without the problem centred discourse currently being employed by the Government (Boseley 2007), allows us to highlight the similarities in drinking practices and discourses articulated by those drinking within guideline rates and hazardous/harmful drinkers. In many ways, hazardous/harmful drinking is not a dangerous behaviour distinct from wider society; it is just an exaggerated form of a widely accepted social practice. Thus, light *and* hazardous/harmful drinkers in our study talked about the importance of alcohol in extra-familial sociability, about its use in winding down, and used discourses about Mediterranean lifestyle to justify their drinking habits. The differences between the groups clearly were evident in terms of level of consumption, but their uses of, and explanations for, their consumption were striking in their similarities, emphasizing that hazardous/harmful drinking is embedded within forms of behaviour widely socially sanctioned in UK society.

The ideological importance of the home (Blunt and Dowling 2006) plays a major role in obscuring this hazardous/harmful domestic drinking. Harmful/hazardous domestic drinkers, though sometimes bingeing in terms of alcohol consumed, are not breaking social or legal rules by being raucous, ill or violent in public space. Rather their actions are entirely consistent with wider social understandings of home: they are using it as a space to unwind, exercising their autonomy in choosing how to do so, and acting as good hosts by making other feel welcome in their home (see Chapter 2). While city centre binge drinking challenges the civility of our streets, domestic drinking can accrue cultural capital to an individual when it is characterized as part of a cultured domestic lifestyle. In this way the contemporary geographical imaginary of binge drinking as a city centre problem (Kneale and French 2008), when set against the positive spatial discourses surrounding the meaning of home (Blunt and Dowling 2006; Laurie et al. 1999), works to obscure the health issues associated with harmful/hazardous domestic drinking. In effect, binge drinking, although technically referring to periods of episodic heavy alcohol consumption, has come in cultural terms to mean dangerous drinking by uncouth youth in the streets of urban Britain. As a result, many of those who consume high levels of alcohol in very different domestic circumstances continue to regard their own practices as unremarkable and feel unwarrantedly insulated from concern.

Chapter 4
Gender

This chapter focuses on the gendered nature of drinking practices. It is almost a truism to state that drinking practices emerge in different ways for men and women, and that responses to their drinking are shaped through a gendered lens of ideas about appropriate masculinities and femininities. Our purpose in this chapter is to study this apparently well accepted fact in order to uncover the ways these practices emerge and form they take in the UK. To pursue this agenda we draw on statistical information from our questionnaire survey and insights from the in-depth interviews. The statistical data gives us a snapshot of contemporary drinking practices, highlighting their gendered nature, but crucially also intra-gender differences between different groups of men, as well as different groups of women. We pursue these gendered patterns, as well as intra-gender variation, through character vignettes from interviewees in Stoke-on-Trent and Eden. These allow us to explore the importance of gendered moralities in shaping drinking practices in public and private locations, and at the same time uncover the significance of other forms of social difference in these diverse drinking cultures.

Masculinities, Femininities and Alcohol Consumption

Government statistics show that drinking is a gendered activity in the UK (Lader and Goddard 2006; Goddard 2008). A recent Omnibus survey, for example, showed that men drink an average of 16 units a week, 66 per cent of which is in the form of beer, lager and cider, 18 per cent wine, 13 per cent spirit, 2 per cent alcopops and 1 per cent fortified wines. Women by contrast average 7 units per week, 43 per cent of which is wine, 25 per cent spirits, and 23 per cent beer, lager and cider, 6 per cent alcopops, and 3 per cent fortified wine. Men's and women's purchasing patterns also show differences in their use of the on-trade, as well as some interesting similarities in aspects of the off-trade. Specifically, men are more likely to purchase alcohol to drink on the premises than are women: 58 per cent of men buy alcohol in licensed bars at least monthly compared with 31 per cent of women; and 33 per cent of men buy alcohol in restaurants at least monthly compared with 23 per cent of women. This gendered pattern carries through to off-licences, which are used by 17 per cent of men and 9 per cent of women on a monthly basis. However, the figures for purchasing alcohol through supermarkets show that 43 per cent of men do so on a monthly basis compared with 40 per cent of women. Indeed, the supermarket is the most common space in which women buy alcohol, as 70 per cent will do so over the course of the year (Lader and Goddard 2006).

Such gendered patterns and practices of alcohol consumption in the Global North are an emerging focus of concern in the geographical literature on drinking, as well as attracting interest in the broader field of alcohol studies. Public drinking spaces, such as the pub, have taken centre stage in this literature. Campbell's (2000) anthropological study of local working men's drinking in a rural New Zealand pub unpicks the competitive sociability of the pub, which he identifies as a key site for the reproduction of hegemonic masculinity. This performance of masculinity in the rural pub requires men to master 'the disciplines of drinking', which here include both the ability to maintain impression of sobriety (e.g. alert conversation, accurate fine motor skills, infrequent urination) after consuming copious amounts of beer, and to display an accumulated knowledge of historical and contemporary local affairs. These disciplines are crucial to success in the dominant mode of interaction, which he terms 'conversational cockfighting', in which men seek to trip up and outwit each other in their nightly discussions of local affairs (see Chapter 2). The masculinity produced is hegemonic but unmarked, as 'pub(lic) masculinity involved not so much a striving towards some defined ideal of masculinity as a desperate struggle to avoid and negate any accusation or appearance of femininity' (Campbell 2000, 576). The consequence is that 'others', most notably women but also men who did not fit this mould, are excluded/excluded themselves from the environment of the pub.

A small number of geographical studies have furthered these arguments about the constitutive performance of masculinity through public drinking, exploring their implications for different groups of men. Leyshon (2005), for example, follows Campbell's lead as he traces the ways in which young men who dominate the backrooms of rural pubs construct and perform hegemonic masculinity. Central to these young men's performance was bodily management in which, for example, they proved they could hold their drink by holding conversations, their bladders and playing pub sports well whilst drinking. This bodily performance, along with phallocentric language and sexist and homophobic discourses mark these as the 'in' young men and relegate other young men and women to marginal areas of the pub, or from it completely. Leyshon (2005) himself notes that 'the ritual is interestingly unrebellious'. Unlike the young people in Kraack and Kenway's (2002) study, who upset older residents by holding parties outside as there were no other places for them to go, these young men reproduce hegemonic masculinity with the landlord's consent and the tactic approval of the older men who occupy the front bar.

In a parallel vein Heley (2008) and Nayak (2003) show how middle-aged and young men's drinking landscapes are cross-cut by class and ethnicity. Heley's (2008) study starts to trace the emergence of a new 'squirearchy', as middle-class male incomers to a rural area seek to position themselves in the local class structure, in part through drinking practices which ape those of farmers they regard as the 'old squires' of the village. This is not a smooth process, both because their interpretation of the class structure is not always shared by locals, and because the economics of the drinks industry are changing rural drinking landscapes. At the other end of the class system, Nayak (2003) traces the ways in which working-class white men from the North East maintain a Geordie identity in the context of deindustrialization. Central to this are hedonistic displays of circuit drinking, which Nayak interprets as a contemporary form of promenading, as well as support for the local football team, as the identity which previous generations of men gained through industrial employment has been replaced by 'its re-enactment through an exaggerated display of white industrial masculinity' in the sphere of consumption (Nayak, 2003, 22; see also Palmer and Thompson, 2007 on alcohol, football supporting and social capital).

This emphasis on the importance of consumption in the contemporary urban experience is equally evident in Latham's (2003) study of Ponsonby, Auckland, New Zealand. Rather than bolstering white industrial masculinity, however, drinking in existing male-orientated haunts has been complemented in this gentrifying area by consumption in a diversity of hospitality establishments (including licensed cafes, hybrid bar/restaurants, etc), which have been self-consciously styled by their owners to challenge existing norms, and to be open to women, as well as a wider diversity of men. What has emerged is a polymorphous public culture, which accommodates a remarkable degree of diversity in terms of gender, ethnicity, sexual orientation and, to a lesser extent, class. This does not materialize through an 'ostentatious celebration of difference', but rather through 'a generalized ethic of benign tolerance, a minimal and usually good humoured acceptance and occasional interest in the diversity of others' (Latham 2003, 1718).

Notwithstanding such radical instances where men and women can challenge, and form alternative identities outside of, existing gender norms, these norms continue to matter, and there is a double standard applied to women's, as opposed to men's, alcohol consumption. Despite the fact that women tend to drink less than men, with fewer consuming to harmful/hazardous levels (Goddard 2008), and the fact that they are less likely to drink drive or be involved in alcohol-related violence, they nevertheless face more opprobrium when they do drink than do men (Plant 1997), and the minority who go on to abuse alcohol 'are seen as less than women' (Ettorre 1997, 2), as 'intrinsically flawed as females' (Waterson 1996, 173). This opprobrium is interesting as it isn't evenly felt over time, rather Waterson (1996) demonstrates that public anxiety about women's drinking peaks in times where their roles are subject to rapid change, most notably during first and second wave feminism. Day et al.'s (2004) analysis of turn of the twenty-first century print media demonstrates that popular interpretations of women's changing drinking patterns remain closely linked with 'traditional' ideas about femininity. Specifically, her analysis shows that media reporting of 'ladette' culture – in which women were represented as aping male behaviour by going out, having a good time, and getting volubly drunk – appeared at the same time as articles which emphasized the threats alcohol played to women's health (in terms of their looks, their fertility, and the health of their unborn child), as well as making them more likely victims of male violence, with men being presented as victims of women who were invading traditionally male domains.

This double standard has had an interesting impact on academic research on research in the Global North. In times where women's drinking has not been deemed an important social issue (e.g. from early 1930s to late 1960s) little was written about it, either in absolute terms or compared with writing on men. When there has been social concern about women's drinking, bio-medical interest in women's drinking during pregnancy dwarfs all other aspects of research, demonstrating 'public attachment to notions of women as child producers and protectors' (Waterson 2000, 7), and widespread concern that '[t]he hand that rocks the cradle should not be a shaky one' (Plant and Plant 2006, 30). Other studies which have sought to understand increases in women's drinking in the latter decades of the twentieth century, tend either to make an argument about women's increased access to alcohol with social change, or to locate problem drinking in the context of difficulties in performing feminine roles, for example dissatisfaction with experiences of motherhood (Waterson 1996). What is missing from this picture is any sense of pleasure women may derive from alcohol (Ettorre 1997), and a broader understanding of how women use alcohol as a part of their everyday life (Waterson 2000). Thus, the double standard in societal responses to men's and women's drinking, although being challenged through feminist work in alcohol studies, has had an enduring influence on the type of academic work undertaken on women and alcohol (Waterson 2000). The movement to challenge the narrowness of the focus on women and drinking in the Global North is still a work in progress in alcohol studies (see Eber 2000, for an alternative focus on the Global South), and is only just starting to emerge in geography, where for example Eldridge and Roberts (2008b) have called for more research into hen parties, and Leyshon (2008) has argued that local pubs are exclusionary spaces for rural young women.

This overview of the emerging geographical literature on alcohol, and its wider academic context, demonstrates that gender is a critical form of social difference in the geographies of alcohol consumption. Public drinking continues to be a key way in which hegemonic forms of masculinity are reproduced and reworked (Heley 2008; Leyshon 2005), and can also be important in sub-cultural responses to changing global-local circumstances (Kraack and Kenway 2002; Latham 2003; Nayak 2003). Although geographical research on women's use of alcohol is rather thin on the ground, isolated studies have started to point to both continuity and change in women's use of public drinking environments (Leyshon 2008; Latham 2003).

To this extent, the geographical literature is starting to offer fascinating insights into the gendering of alcohol consumption. In this chapter, however, we want to address two current lacunae in this field: the relative paucity of research on women and gender (as opposed to men), and the dearth of research considering private as well as public drinking environments (Holloway 2008; Kneale and French 2008). We begin by using our statistical data to pick out gendered patters in men's and women's drinking in different environments, and then explore the ways their drinking flows between supposedly public and private environment through a focus on individual men and women.

Gendered Drinking Patterns, Places and Purposes

Our survey results demonstrate some broad ranging variations in men's and women's drinking practices (see Holloway et al. 2009, for more details). Men, as the literature might lead us to suspect (Goddard 2008; Lader and Goddard 2006), drink more than women (see Table 4.1). Men are also significantly more likely to drink in pubs than are women, a fact which demonstrates that the emphasis in the literature on pubs as spaces for the reproduction of masculinity is crucial (Campbell 2000; Nayak 2003; Leyshon 2005). However, even as the statistics confirm men's greater use of the pub, they also point to potential ruptures in the longstanding association between public drinking and less 'respectable' women (Plant 1997; Day et al. 2004; Plant and Plant 2006), as the majority of women also report drinking in this space. The fact that significantly greater numbers of women than men drink regularly in restaurants and friends'/family's homes, also highlights the need to consider drinking in more diverse public and quasi public/private drinking environments if we want fully to explore the gendered geographies of alcohol consumption. Perhaps the most striking statistics in Table 4.1, however, and much less remarked upon in wider popular and policy debates about drinking in the early twenty-first century (Plant and Plant 2006), is that the most popular drinking venue with both men and women is their own home (Holloway et al. 2008).

If we look at the reasons why people drink, there are some important gender differences but these do not obscure the degree of commonality between gender groups. As Table 4.1 shows, significantly more men do report drinking to relax and to get drunk than do women (a pattern in line with national data – Lader and Goddard 2006). However, these differences are no more important than are the similarities between the genders: over 70 per cent of men and women rated taste, sociability and relaxation as reasons for drinking, whereas less than 25 per cent of both genders reported getting drunk, losing one's inhibitions or family/peer pressure as reasons for drinking.

The relative simplicity of this picture – in which men drink more than women, preferring subtly different locations, but largely drinking for similar purposes – is disturbed somewhat when we look at intra-gender variation. Age is a crucial factor for both genders. Young men and women are significantly more likely to drink to a higher level than their older counterparts, and are more likely to frequent pubs and clubs. However, given the amount of negative press attention young women's drinking has received in the past decade (Day et al. 2004), it is worth remembering that more young men drink above 'harmful levels' than young women. Nevertheless, young men and women share very similar drinking motivations, and the final three reasons for drinking discussed above – getting drunk, losing one's inhibitions and family/peer pressure – are significantly more

Table 4.1   Gender and Drinking Level, Location and Motivation (%)

Drinking levels in Previous Week

	None	Within guidelines	Hazardous drinking	Harmful drinking
Men	**33.5**	**43.2**	**16.8**	**6.5**
Women	**46.9**	37.7	11.8	**3.6**

Regular Drinking Locations

	Pubs	Clubs	Restaurants	Friends'/family's	Own home
Men	**66.8**	23.9	49.5	60.3	74.0
Women	**51.9**	21.4	56.0	66.7	71.8

Reasons for drinking alcohol

	I like the taste	To be sociable	To relax	To get drunk	To loosen my inhibitions	As a reward	Peer/family pressure
Men	86.0	86.7	**80.1**	**23.8**	25.4	23.9	7.0
Women	86.2	85.0	**73.4**	**16.9**	21.3	22.7	7.7

Source: Authors' questionnaire survey

Notes: **Bold type** = significant at 5 per cent level; normal type = not significant at 5 per cent level.

common amongst younger people than their older counterparts. For example, 74 per cent and 53 per cent of 18–24 year old men and women (respectively) cite getting drunk as a reason for drinking, compared with only 11 per cent and 2 per cent of the 55–64 year old age group.

Age is not the only factor shaping different drinking attitudes and practices within the gender categories. Religious affiliation appears to be an inhibitory/protective factor in both men's and women's drinking, with significantly more men and women with no religion drink to higher levels than do religious males and females. These differences in drinking levels reflect differences in drinking motivation. Religious belief appears to exclude/protect both men and women from hedonism: significantly more non-religious men reported drinking to relax and to get drunk than their religious counterparts, while significantly more non-religious women reported drinking to get drunk and lose their inhibitions than did religious women. A focus on the much less studied public drinking environment of the restaurant, and the private space of the home, reminds us that class-based conventions also shape our drinking landscapes (Lader and Goddard 2006). Higher socio-economic class is associated with a greater propensity to drink in these environments amongst men and women. Moreover, there are hints in the statistical data that local cultures are a factor in shaping drinking motivations (which would go some way towards explaining regional variations in drinking patterns – Lader and Goddard 2006). For example, women in Stoke-on-Trent, an urban environment where more women were visible in the public drinking environments of the pub and restaurants, were significantly more likely to report family/peer pressure as reasons for drinking than were women in rural Eden.

Gendered Drinking Vignettes

In this section we want to add some flesh to the bones of our argument that gender differences continue to matter in men's and women's drinking patterns, places and purposes, but that these gendered practices are also cross-cut with other lines of social differentiation. Our approach here to provide a number of character vignettes, and show how the drinking practices of these individuals were shaped by gendered drinking moralities, moralities which were subtly, and not so subtly, reflective of other aspects of their social positioning. The range of vignettes we produces here is far from exhaustive (see Holloway et al. 2009, for alternatives) but each has been chosen to illustrate different elements of processes we saw at work in our study.

Melissa: Young Women's Fun and Heterosexed Control

We begin by introducing Melissa Worthington, who was 18 at the time we interviewed her and living in rural Eden (NS-SEC 2). Melissa, like many young people, first started drinking illicitly in her mid-teens, in her case drinking vodka in a secluded spot by the river Eden, and moving on to drink in local venues when she looked old enough to 'pass' as 18. For her drinking alcohol was partly a rebellion against the limited nature of the rural area in which she lives: she drank to liven up life in the 'boring' rural area which has very limited social opportunities for teenagers (Valentine et al. 2008). The bodily feelings alcohol induces are also a key attraction. Whilst describing herself as shy in most parts of her life, she explains that alcohol 'loosens' her up and when she goes out drinking she is loud and sociable (see Chapter 7). Although she continues to 'binge drink' at weekends, her self-identification of a sensible young woman who wants to do well at school and go away to University, along with the fact that drinking is now legal and therefore less exciting, means she limits her consumption during the week:

> It's like now you're allowed to do it, what's the point, you know what I mean, it's like oh well I'm allowed to go and get it, there's no fun in it now. ... That was the whole fun of it.

Melissa's drinking history to date has clearly been shaped by the rural environment within which she lives. The processes through which she gained access to public drinking environments such as bars and clubs, and the way she continues to negotiate these, demonstrate the importance of gendered, and heterosexed, control on women's behaviour. Melissa's parents were happy to let her go to the pub as an under-aged teen as she went in the company of her older brother. He was there to monitor her behaviour: if she got a little drunk 'he kind of covered for me', but would intervene to stop her drinking if he thought her too drunk, as she explains: 'if he sees I am getting in a state or whatever, he'll say right now, come on'. This form of supervision was not, however, provided altruistically by her brother, as she was aware he was happy to take her to the pub because she would be of interest to his male friends:

> it's like, you get to that age and all his friends are like hovering round you and oh who's this? Because I'm the new girl type thing, so he wants me to go out, to like talk to them and ...

The contemporary drinking practices Melissa describes, though involving 'binge drinking' in terms of the amount of alcohol consumed, do not nearly align with media images of drunk women spilling out of super pubs and clubs and then fighting on the streets late at night in our towns and cities (Plant and Plant 2006). Rather she describes a situation in which men dominate at the bar and move actively around a venue, whilst women are more likely to drinking in groups at a table, and only approach the bar in the company of other women:

> I wouldn't go by myself [to the bar] ... when lads are drinking they're normally stood up hovering around the bar, but when we drink we sit down ... 'cos like

the lads are always moving about the places but we just like our little corner and we just sit there and people gather around us.

Moreover, this wider gendered pattern in the use of space in pubs and clubs, which means women play a more sedentary role in rural public drinking environments, is reinforced through her interpersonal relations as a heterosexual young woman. To expand, whilst Melissa is happy to get volubly drunk with her friends she seeks to limit her drinking in front of her boyfriend in order to conform to regulative models of appropriate gendered and heterosexed behaviour, and avoid the sanctions which might result if she broke these:

Well usually I go out with my friends beforehand, so that's when I, you know I get really drunk, and then I meet up with him later and I kind of, when I meet up with him, I kind of stop drinking from then on. I've had enough anyway but I just don't want to make a fool of myself in front of him. Get told off.

Claire: A Responsible Mother

Claire Hall is 24 (NS-SEC 5) and her early drinking experiences have some parallels with those of Melissa. At 14 she started going to the pub with her 17-year-old boyfriend to play pool and drink lemonade. She describes herself as rebellious at this time, but her mother's attempts to discipline her and prevent her from going to the pub were subverted by the landlord of the pub, who argued that she wasn't drinking alcohol and was causing no trouble. In a rural context where there was no other venue for young people to meet Claire continued to visit the pub, progressing from the backroom to the front room of the pub when her boyfriend (who she later married) became old enough to drink alcohol. Claire was in her early 30s when we interviewed her and is no longer a regular pub-goer:

I work full-time and it gets to the weekend and I really don't want to start getting ready to go out. [I] just want to snuggle down and sit in front of the fire and grow old.

At first sight it would simply seem as though Claire has moved through the age-related patterns revealed in our survey, where younger people are more likely to visit public drinking venues while more of their older counterparts slip into domestic patterns of life. To simply interpret this only as an age-related pattern would be inaccurate though. Her gender identity, and in particular her vision of herself as a good mother, has been central in shaping her drinking practices. As she explains, she stopped going to the pub when she had her first child at 19 in order to prove that she was a good mother (Waterson 1996; Ettorre 1997; Plant and Plant 2006):

I had my daughter when I was 19 ... so that put life on hold because I was determined to be a good mother, I wasn't going to let anybody say I couldn't because I was 19. So I think really, going to town and everything was just [something I started to do again] like a couple of years ago when I was 30, you know, I've done my, you know I've done a fairly good job.

However, this desire to be seen as a good mother is not just a performance she puts on for others, an effort to keep up appearances; it is also something central to her self-identity. It shapes her domestic drinking practices, meaning both that she drinks little (although not nothing) at home herself, and also tries to steer her husband away from domestic drinking:

I mean my husband, you know he, although he hasn't for a while actually, but he went through a phase of you know he'd go up the street and buy 4 cans of lager in the middle of the week and I'd be like why are you buying them and it was just, you know, quite, and I think that's because I've got the kids and I've got this thing that they see him drinking and they're going to grow up and do [it]. And I do, I do think that you get so protective over, and I think that's what I've been trying to do is be this model mum.

Bazid: Becoming an Abstemious Family Man

Bazid Nazar is 23 (NS-SEC 4) and has experience of moving into a phase of life centred on family and childrearing has some parallels, but also contrasts, with that of Claire. As a young man in college in Stoke-on-Trent, Bazid started getting drunk in parks and clubs with a group of male Muslim friends. Like many of the young people in our survey he drank to get drunk, to loosen his inhibitions and to help him socialize (see also Orford et al. 2004):

... drink helps you to relax more, I think that's the reason probably why I drunk I think, because it just helped you relax and you know socialize with other people, some people who you probably wouldn't never talk to, especially even when it comes to girls ...

Bazid's experience of this process was shaped by his religion (see Chapter 5). As a Muslim, he felt the need to hide his drinking both from his family and wider members of his religious community (Bradby 2007; Orford et al. 2004). He later progressed on to use of pubs in the company of mixed gender 'English' friends (his term), a process that was facilitated by their cultural knowledge of pubs, and partly motivated by his desire to fit in and be accepted by them. Other than at point of entry or exit, drinking in pubs also kept him hidden from the wider Muslim community, whilst more pleasantly sheltered from the elements.

Much of Bazid's drinking as a very young man was highly enjoyable, involving relaxing with friends and success with women; however, he gradually started to drink to excess in an attempt to manage stress (see Burns et al. 2002; Brickell 2008):

> I was just drinking to, well I don't know, keep my head above water really, and just you know, stay stress free and I think that made me feel a lot worse mentally.

Eventually, one of his friends sought to intervene:

> [H]e said: "You're drinking too much, you're drinking for the wrong reasons, you're just drinking 'cos you're stressed out or you know, you're upset about certain things, it's not right" and so on … I was glad he did and that gave me a focus on trying to stop drinking.

Although he labels this specific intervention as his trigger to stop drinking, Bazid also articulates the ways in which his experience of drinking as a very young man, but then growing out of it in his twenties and settling down to married and family life earlier than 'English' friends is a pattern common amongst his male Muslim peers (see Bradby 2007, on Muslim, Sikh and Hindu young people). This is a process which has changed his priorities:

> I think when you do seem to get married a lot, obviously at an early age and you have children your responsibilities and your… main focus on life completely changes then, it's not about getting a drink, it's about making sure you've got a roof over your head and got food on the table and looking after your kids.

Bazid is now a committed non-drinker, and as a man in his twenties, with his eldest child under 5, most of his sociability is family based. While this lifestyle is validated within his religious community, it is nevertheless something which can mark him out as 'other' in the factory where he works. Notwithstanding this workplace peer pressure, he is resolute that drinking now, after several years of not doing so, would be letting himself down.

Rob: A Regular at his Local Pub

Rob Edgerton is part of the pattern, highlighted by the survey, in which men are more likely to drink in pubs than women (Lader and Goddard 2006). For Rob, a white, retired professional/managerial worker (65+) from Stoke-on-Trent, drinking is about sociability. He goes to the pub with someone, or on the off-chance that someone he knows will be there, and does not drink at home where he lives alone. The amount of alcohol he consumes sometimes affects his bodily abilities, but he explains that while he feels foolish if he can not walk in a straight line, some form of 'self-preservation takes over' and that he simply 'bounces off fences' on his journey home. At the time we met him, concern about the amount he was drinking had recently caused him to cut down from 7 to 3 or 4 visits a week, drinking a couple of pints on most visits, but occasionally binge drinking.

Rob's concerns about his drinking are not overtly moral in nature. He is a not religious, a group of men the survey showed used pubs more than others (see also Michalak et al. 2007), and the drinking community of which he is a part is relatively accepting of drunkenness. In contrast to previous studies which emphasized the importance of man's ability to hold his drink to hegemonic masculinity (Campbell 2000; Leyshon 2005), responses to inebriation in Rob's local are both kindly and a measure of belonging, as those who are "part of the crowd" might be driven home by the landlord or walked home by other customers. There is for Rob a mismatch between this relatively accepting attitude to drunkenness, and his own sense that the following hangover is wasteful:

> So you'd think blimey I've had, I've had eight pints. Then you find the next day literally you just couldn't operate ... the day's a write off. You know, you'd got plans to do things but you just couldn't, couldn't be bothered ... and you think that's not right, it's a waste, it's a waste of a day.

Rob's efforts to cut down on his drinking are, however, tempered by the importance of the pub in his social life. There is a tension in his account between resisting the desire to be there too much, and fearing that he will be forgotten if he stays away for too long. On the one hand, he claims he no longer feels the need to go every night in case he misses what people are talking about; on the other, he still ensures he visits sufficiently regularly to remain part of this community. Indeed, it is this sense of community, the pub's importance as a space of sociability and support (cf. Laurier and Philo 2006, on cafés), rather than simply conversational cockfighting (cf. Campbell 2000), which makes not drinking an unrealistic prospect for Rob:

> I'd love to have been the sort of person who didn't drink.... I don't have to drink but the other side is the sort of camaraderie that's, that you, you sort of miss out on, ... it's like a sort of camaraderie and it's also a sort of mutual thing ... there's always help, you know, and advice ... like little jobs that people, say like I need this doing and oh, you know, do this, sort you out, I'll get you this, I'll get you that ... You do this, I'll do that, ... you know sort of exchange and barter ... So there's always ... community of sort of whatsits that people ... look out for you and ... provide you with things and ... make suggestions and, and advice. And so if I didn't drink, if I didn't do it, I would ... miss out on ... that.

Conclusion

The results of the mixed-methods research presented above reveal continuing evidence of 'traditional' differences between men and women in terms of their drinking levels, locations and motivations, as well as potential notes of change. For example, the survey demonstrates that men are more likely to drink in pubs than are women, but also that a majority of women too frequent these drinking environments. If we contrast Rob's experience of being a regular in his local pub and the social support he receives through this, with Melissa's experience of gaining entry into this world in the company of her brother and boyfriend, as well as in all female groups, we can elucidate some of the ways in which these general patterns of inclusion and exclusion work out in the lives of individuals.

Focusing on gender difference in this way allows us to explore the importance of gendered moralities in shaping different social practices (Tolvanen and Jylhä 2005). Rob's and Melissa's decisions about pub use were not individual choices made in a vacuum, but were shaped to some extent by the communities of which they were a part. Rob wanted to go to the pub because this was the location in which it was considered socially appropriate for men to meet. Melissa was able to access this at a young age as her brother was cast as carer, however, when old enough to access it in her own right her experience continued to be gendered in terms of her use of space within venues, and in terms of maintaining respectable femininity in the presence of her boyfriend. Such findings demonstrate that gender continues to matter, even as the meanings and practices associated with this socially constituted category continue to change.

Crucially, the findings from the mixed-methods research also demonstrate the impossibility of fully understanding gender difference without considering the ways in which men and women of different ages, social class, and religion experience gender. The survey data, for example, demonstrates that age and religion matter to both genders, with younger and non-religious men and women drinking more than their older and religious counterparts, and often for more hedonistic reasons.

The character vignettes add texture and depth to this argument. Contrasting Melissa's experience with that of Claire demonstrates that these heterosexed gendered moralities are not uniformly experienced by all women rather they are constituted in different ways for women of different ages and at different points in the 'lifecourse'. So whilst Melissa is seeking to negotiate respectable heterosexual femininity in the pub, for Claire the ideologies surrounding motherhood, and in particular her desire to be seen as, and judge herself to be, a good mother meant removing herself from the pub, as well as limiting her domestic drinking. These are both gendered moralities, involving as they do judgements about the ways 'good' women behave, but the standard against which Melissa and Claire were judged, and judge themselves, reflected their different positions in the lifecourse.

Religion too is an important feature of these vignettes, though it is easier to see when the individual hold religious beliefs that in its absence. Rob, for example, enjoyed the sociability of the pub, and as a non-religious man belongs to the group of men more likely to use these venues. His concerns about the amount he drinks, and in particular the waste of time in which hangovers result, are marked by the absence rather than the presence of religious doctrine overt concern about the morality or 'evils of drink' (see Chapter 1). Bazid, by contrast, linked his changing drinking practices to a reorientation towards family life. His example demonstrates that gendered moralities, in this case what it is means to be a good man, husband and father, can also be overtly shaped by the belief communities of which people are a part. His determination to abstain from alcohol was not a process of judging himself against some generic vision of manhood, it was shaped in relation to ideas about being a good Muslim man.

In addition to revealing continuity and change in the gendering of drinking practices, the mixed-method approach employed in this research also allows us to fulfil our second aim – to explore a diversity of public and private drinking environments (Kneale and French 2008). Much of the previous literature had been concerned with the pub as a site for the reproduction of masculinity (Campbell 2000; Leyshon 2005; Heley 2008). This is indeed an important issue, with the survey showing this to be the most popular drinking environment amongst men, and the case-study men illustrating the diverse roles it can play in their lives, including acting as a site of community and social support for Rob, and being a space in which he could fit in with his 'English' friends and hide away from the wider Muslim community for Bazid (cf. Bradby 2007). However, the survey also shows that people's own homes (Holloway et al. 2008), and for women friends' and family's homes, and restaurants are more popular drinking environments than the pub. Claire's vignette starts to point to some of the complex meanings domestic alcohol consumption can have. On the one hand for her it is a private space away from the pub where her behaviour will not be judged by others; on the other hand her own ideas about good parenting means she seeks to limit her own drinking, and that of her husband, in this space.

Chapter 5
Ethnicity

In contrast to a voluminous amount of research in North America it has been noted that there is relatively little writing focused on ethnic minorities and alcohol consumption in Europe (Harrison et al. 1996). In the UK for example, work has focused on describing the prevalence and remission rates of alcohol dependence, counting levels of mortality, assessing service utilization and treatment effectiveness as well as some attempts to consider drinking practices amongst different ethnic groups – African-Caribbean, Indian, Chinese, Pakistani. Sikh, Hindu, Irish (Heim et al. 2004; Harrison 1996; Cochrane and Bal 1990; Mckeigue and Karmi 1993, Harrison and Carr-Hill 1992). Given the paucity of research there is of course significant and wide-ranging opportunities to engage with the complex and diverse geographies of alcohol, drinking and drunkenness amongst and between different ethnic groups in different spaces and places. Here, we focus on developing a detailed understanding of the role of alcohol in the lives of Muslims in Stoke-on-Trent. In particular, we use the lens of a culture of abstention to provide a new perspective on debates about access to public space and social cohesion in the contemporary urban night-time economy.

The Muslim Culture of Abstinence

While studying alcohol, drinking and drunkenness has provided fertile terrain for geographers, much less attention has been paid to cultures of abstention (with the exception of historical work on temperance e.g. Kneale 2001) and the implications of the importance of alcohol in urban regeneration for non-drinkers' willingness to participate in night-time economies. However, research suggests that 13 per cent of the UK population *do not* have an alcoholic drink during the course of a year (Lader and Goddard 2006). Alongside some Christian denominations all the main religions in South Asia condemn the use of alcohol, although in practice it is only among Muslims that abstinence is widespread (Ghost 1984; McKeigue and Karmi 1993). Here, we explore Muslim attitudes and alcohol- related practices within the community. In doing so we focus on consideration of how the Muslim community's culture of abstention shapes its members access to, and use of, space. In doing so, we follow Latham and McCormack (2004) in foregrounding the active role played by alcohol, as a non human actor, in shaping emergent social relations by exploring its agency in generating social fissures and producing new exclusions.

According to the most recent national census Muslims are the single largest religious minority in the UK with a population of 1.6 million (ONS 2003), although this figure is regarded as likely to be a conservative estimate of the actual current population. The majority of British Muslims are of South Asian origin, although this is not to suggest that the community is homogenous, rather it is bisected by cultural, language and doctrinal differences (Berns McGown 1999; Hasan 2001; Ahmed 2003). Muslims are often located within an imagined Black or Asian community yet define themselves first, and foremost, in relation to their faith, rather than their race, ethnicity or nationalities (Modood 1992; Valentine and Sporton 2009). As such religious values are integral to the Muslim community (Werbner 1990). Islam is what Yip (2004) defines as a 'total system', guiding Muslims individually and collectively in all aspects of their everyday life. As such, this faith also powerfully shapes the time-space routines of both practising individuals and the rhythms of communities (e.g. through the rituals of prays, visits to the Mosque, Qur'anic education classes and so on). Indeed, the *Qur'an* is widely believed to be the literal word of God and therefore not to be open to change or compromise.

Islam forbids the consumption of alcohol, although it does not provide a specific rationalization for this tenet of the faith, and therefore as these interviewees explain, like most Muslims, they do not drink regardless of the positive or negative impacts of alcohol in wider society:

> Islam has it's own, culture, it's an ideological base, and part of that ideological base is that you don't drink, it's completely forbidden, it's a rule, it's a law [edit] The, the code of life that I follow is Islam, so what's legal and what's illegal is defined by the *Qu'ran* and it defines alcohol as illegal that's why I don't drink alcohol. [edit] I think it's an advantage all the time, I believe it's going to get you to paradise you see, and that's very advantageous.
>
> (Afzul Mohammed, Stoke-on-Trent, 45–54, Male, NS-SEC 4)

> It's forbidden because Allah says that it's forbidden, there's no reason, there's no...specific reasons given. Allah says that it's forbidden and therefore it is forbidden. We don't participate in drinking alcohol, despite the, the fact of what you see in society, how it causes problems in society, that's not the reasons from Islam, why it's forbidden. It's forbidden and that is that. But you can see the after effects of alcohol, people, people, alcoholics, the after effects in society, with the problems that it causes, as reasons for not drinking, but when you're talking, when you're referring it back to Islam, we don't drink because Allah forbids it ... [I] abide by the rules, what is allowed and what isn't allowed and it's not allowed to drink, so I don't drink.
>
> (Simi Altaf, Stoke-on-Trent, 25–34, Male, NS-SEC 4).

This culture of abstinence is regulated by social obligation. Within British Muslim communities close-knit family networks produce strong expectations of integration and conformity, particularly for first generation immigrants (Dwyer 1999; Valentine et al. 2009). Maintaining family honour (*izzat*) and respect towards parents and elders are regarded as important elements of the faith (Norcliffe 1999). The *Qur'an*, *Shari'ah* and *Hadith* all stress familial duties and hierarchal familial relations (Modood and Berthoud 1997; Zokaei and Phillips 2000). Indeed, Yip (2004) points out that a third of the legal injunctions in the *Qur'an* relate to marriage and the family, setting out how these relationships should be managed and regulated. Likewise, amongst Pakistani Muslims *biradari* (literal meaning brotherhood) refers to extended clan or tribal networks and allegiances which provide support and a sense of solidarity for members, but also carry with them a set of social obligations and expectations. In this way, because the community has shared values or norms in relation to abstinence its social network serves to monitor and regulate its members' behaviour. Coleman (1988, 106) refers to this type of process by which a social group, such as a faith community (i.e. where parents are friends of the parents of their children's friends), supports and reinforces the ability of parents' to socialize their children into its 'norms' and to strengthen their commitment to its value system as 'intergenerational closure'. Previous geographical research for example, has demonstrated how the Muslim community works in this way to regulate young women's dress and other aspects of their embodied identities (Dwyer 1999; Valentine et al. 2009). Similar processes are evident in relation to the consumption of alcohol (cf. Bradby 2007) as this interviewee explains:

> There's no formal structure of policing, but there's people who kind, there's Islam core within each community who go out and their presence usually prevents drinking.
>
> (Afzul Mohammed, Stoke-on-Trent, 45–54, Male, NS-SEC 4)

In particular, because the Muslim community is concentrated in specific neighbourhoods, and many of taxi drivers who operate in the city centre are from the Pakistani community, there is a sense that the eyes of the community are always on the street. This fact of potentially being able always to be seen meant that some of the interviewees who were tempted to drink described exercising self-discipline in what is, in effect, a Foucauldian sense (Foucault 1977). Indeed, some of the Muslim respondents described the sense of pride they feel in their ability to resist the temptation to drink and in the discipline of their faith, as well as observing the financial and health benefits of abstinence.

Latham and McCormack (2004, 717) have argued that alcohol has agency in that 'the affects of alcohol are implicated in particular forms of sociality, of ways of being and relating through the urban, ways of moving, gesturing, walking and talking variously identifiable as drunkenness and intoxication'. As we shall see in Chapter 7 the ability of alcohol to heighten affective intensities in a variety of ways enables drinkers to relax, have fun, lose their inhibitions and so on. Yet, for those Muslims who do not drink, alcohol has the reverse impact on structures of feeling, generating emotions of disgust and repulsion. Interviewees who had limited exposure to drinking often described the taste of alcohol as unpleasant rather than in terms of generating feelings of pleasure and relaxation. More generally, the comments of those who do not drink indicated a dislike of the power of alcohol as an independent agent to make people act in ways that they would not normally, in particular by changing pleasant, respectable, individuals into loud, out of control, child-like figures. Such behaviour runs counter to cultural expectations of modesty and embodied respectability. Other informants described how because alcohol is a 'confidence booster' it can make people act in assertive or aggressive ways which can generate conflict and violence amongst normally law-abiding citizens:

> Just makes you talk nonsense basically, some you know, could make you violent…our religion clearly telling us no drinking and I understand why because it makes you, basically makes you do things that you wouldn't normally do, makes you say things that you normally wouldn't say because of the drink…it takes you total out of character depending on how much you've had…so you're not going to respect people after you've had a certain amount, you won't respect people.
>
> (Farooq Hussain, Stoke-on-Trent, 25–34, Male, NS-SEC 2)

Of course, as with any faith, everyday practices do not always adhere to religious proscriptions. Despite a culture of abstinence nonetheless some Pakistani Muslims still experiment with, or regularly drink, alcohol. In the following section we reflect on the role of alcohol as an absent presence within the Pakistani Muslim community.

An Absent Presence: Alcohol in the Pakistani Muslim Community

All of our interviewees acknowledged that there are significant levels of alcohol consumption within the local Pakistani Muslim community despite the religious prohibitions on drinking. This finding mirrors the evidence of other research dating back over two decades. For example, a health survey conducted in Wolverhampton, UK, which included questions about alcohol consumption, found that 56 per cent of the respondents who self-identified as Muslims reported drinking alcohol (Johnson 1987 personal communication cited in Cochrane and Bal 1990). Likewise, in a study of alcohol consumption in Southall, London, UK, although alcohol consumption was lower amongst Muslim men than any other of the other social groups surveyed, 20 per cent of the Pakistani and Indian Muslim respondents reported drinking alcohol at least once a week (McKeigue and Karmi 1993). More strikingly, a community survey of 800 men in the UK, randomly sampled from Sikh, Muslim, Hindu and white English-born majority populations (200 men from each group, matched for age), found that while the Muslim men had the lowest reported level of alcohol consumption, the few who did drink consumed more alcohol on average than the other groups. Indeed, the Muslims who were regular drinkers and aged 41–50 consumed the second highest number of units of alcohol of all population and age groups in the sample (Cochrane and Bal 1990). While the figures for actual levels of consumption are highly variable between these studies – perhaps reflecting problems inherent in conducting alcohol surveys (Goddard 2001) – nonetheless they provide clear evidence that alcohol is an issue within Muslim communities notwithstanding the cultural tradition of abstinence.

The evidence of our study however, highlights that patterns of consumption within the Pakistani Muslim community are gendered and generational. In particular, drinking is an activity largely confined to young men. From the interviewees' accounts of their own, or observations of others', behaviour a common pattern appears to be that young men start drinking in their mid to late teens. It is well established through social studies of childhood and youth that peer groups are a key influence on young people's risk-taking behaviours (including not only drinking but also smoking, gambling, and under age sex) which represent an inherent part of the process of making the transition from childhood to adulthood (e.g. Plant and Plant 1992; Parker et al. 1998; Hoffman et al. 2003; Chatterton and Hollands 2003; Nairn et al. 2006). Indeed, for children, contemporary status within their own peer groups is often more important to them than adult concerns about their education or future health and well-being (Valentine et al. 2002). James' (1993) qualitative research demonstrates that young people in managing their peer group relationships commonly walk a tight-rope between 'conformity' and 'individuality', in other words behaving like others in order to fit in with the group, while at the same time contributing something different that makes them valued. While Jones and Jones (2000) argue that problematic or social behaviour is 'contagious' because 'influential friends' legitimize these activities and enrol others into them through processes including goading, coercion and competitiveness. All of the Pakistani Muslim interviewees in this study described encountering such peer pressures to drink in order to belong and be accepted. Indeed, most noted the integral role that drinking spaces such as pubs and clubs (and their associated social drinking rituals) play in young people's social, as well as workplace, networks. While some of the informants had resisted (and indeed continue to resist pressures from colleagues and acquaintances to drink in order to fit in), those interviewees who do drink or had previously experimented with alcohol, described doing so because of the agency of alcohol to transform their self-confidence – particularly for young men in relation to talking to young women – to generate a sense of belonging, and because it effected an escape from the stresses and regulation of everyday family life.

Yet, at the same time, they acknowledged that in doing so alcohol also induced feelings of guilt about the implications of doing so in relation to their faith and family:

I think drink, although yeah, it's not allowed in our religion ... it's not good for your health and so on, but one thing it is, it makes you more sociable ... I think 'cos drink helps you to relax more, I think that's the reason probably why I drunk I think, because it just helped you relax and you know socialise with other people, some people who you probably wouldn't never talk to, especially even when it comes to girls I suppose, you know what I mean, sometimes you'd be a bit shy or whatever, once you'd had a couple of drinks down you there was nothing stopping you ... [Describing his first experience of drinking alcohol] I felt guilty because in the back of my mind I always knew that what I was doing was wrong and but with all my friends doing it and with all the influence from them as well [Edit] I don't know, I think we just started to think it was a bit more socially acceptable for some reason, and we knew it wasn't but we probably just thought that because some of the friends that we hang around, hung around with at the time were English and for them it's acceptable anyway so I think you know, probably in the back of our minds we wanted to be accepted for us.

(Bazid Nazar, Stoke-on-Trent, 25–34, Male, NS-SEC 3)

Drinking by women however is much more strongly prohibited and policed by families and the wider Pakistani Muslim community than that by young men. This mirrors the more general regulation of women's bodies and identities (Dwyer 1999; Valentine et al. 2009; Bradby 2007), which is facilitated by the physical and emotional proximity of family and kin, and close-knit nature of social life within Muslim communities. It was only by leaving home and going away to University in another part of the country that one female informant created the space to experiment with alcohol. The costs of transgressing normative codes of behaviour are also potentially more severe for women. Bradby's (2007) study of the British Asian community in Glasgow for example, reports the experience of a young woman who is no longer considered marriageable in her community because she has been seen on 'nights out' with friends who are drinking, despite the fact that she herself was not drinking alcohol:

I think that with a lot of parents, especially with boys, it would be a case of ask no questions, hear no lies, but with girls it's definitely, definitely taboo and you'd actually, a lot of Asian girls, and I think I'm probably the exception rather than the rule, aren't, don't really have the freedoms to be able to go and do it in the first place unless they go to university and they're away from home.

(Uddin Masood, Stoke-on-Trent, 25–34, Male, NS-SEC 3)

I think definitely if it's known that a girl's drinking, if a girl's drinking she'll get it from all sides, like the guys will look at her, the younger guy drinkers will look at her in a funny way, all the people, I think they see some disdain towards drinking but they do overlook their sons drinking it, their daughters doing it she'll be whisked off to Pakistan.

(Afzul Mohammed, Stoke-on-Trent, 45–54, Male, NS-SEC 4)

Those of our informants who do drink described explicitly doing so to get drunk. The most common drinks consumed are spirits bought from off-licences. These are usually drunk in informal spaces (such as the park, in cars, bus shelters etc.) rather than at home or public space because of the risk of being seen doing so by family or community members and therefore bringing shame on both the drinker and their family (although some informants did describe taking the risk of going to public venues in parts of the city not frequented by the Pakistani community and to one venue owned by a young Asian entrepreneur who could be trusted to protect their 'secret'). This pattern of alcohol consumption contrasts with that by white majority informants in the same age groups who, as well as drinking regularly in public venues, also exhibit significant levels of domestic consumption (Holloway et al. 2008a):

Farooq: A lot of, lot of young people do it ... They do it secretive with their mates, yeah, they're not going to do it in the open because they're Muslims, you know bad thing, you know they get highlighted ...

Interviewer: So where do you think they do it then?

Farooq: Parked up in cars. Out in colleges. Where nobody can see them, anywhere where they think they can't get caught.
(Farooq Hussain, Stoke-on-Trent, 25–34, Male, NS-SEC 2)

The interviewees who drink, or had drunk in the past, recounted various strategies that they have used to conceal their drinking from their parents. This secrecy was rationalized in terms of both the importance of respecting parents within the Muslim faith and therefore not troubling them with something of which they would disapprove, and/or because drinking was argued to be a private matter that should not be the concern of others: Nonetheless, despite the informants' ability to justify their drinking practices the consumption of alcohol has the effect of producing strong emotions of guilt as this interviewee describes:

I can remember ... I used to walk my mate's home [where they would drink together] ... it's about what, three quarters of a mile, it's not far, it's ten, fifteen minute walk, but it used to feel like the longest walk ever, it felt like it was lasting for days and days. I was going home right, and I was thinking right okay, am I sober? Am I [walking] straight? Is anyone going to be up at home and so on? And you know I used to walk home and look to see if there was a light on, and if I'd see a light on downstairs, I used to just walk around the streets for a bit and just wait for the light to go off then just creep in the house and go straight to bed. So it was just that walking home was I think, it was more a feeling of, probably guilt, I've had a good night, I've had a brilliant night, I've really

enjoyed myself and now it was time to back down, come back down to reality
now. I think it was just a guilt trip like, really, walking home.

(Haidar Ahmed, Stoke-on-Trent, 16–24, Male, NS SEC 4)

The interviewees were divided as to the longer term implications of young
Pakistani Muslim men experimenting with alcohol. For some, it represented a
generational shift in attitude and behaviour. Notably, those who abstained from
drinking regarded alcohol consumption within the Pakistani Muslim community
as a negative product of integration (i.e. as the interviewee below comments:
'drinking is part of the British way of life'), and in effect, as marking a discontinuity
or break with the community's collective male traditions, and a slippage into more
individualized ways of being that are characteristic of contemporary UK society
(Giddens 1991). Indeed, one interviewee credited alcohol with the agency to
provide a significant threat to the Muslim faith:

> Yeah, there's definitely intergenerational differences, because our parents, kind
> of [come] from a Pakistani cultural perspective, ie we've been told not to drink
> so we mustn't … Young people obviously like I said, the whole integration
> model of society that you can sit in a pub but not drink, really should integrate,
> really should be part of the British way of life. But, I believe environment, I
> know from personal experience and you can see from society around you, that
> environment is the most influencing factor … it's the environment that they live
> in that moulds their, their personality, so that integration model definitely leads
> to people drinking.

(Afzul Mohammed, Stoke-on-Trent, 45–54, Male, NS-SEC 4)

However, none of those who drank alcohol, or had previously experimented
with drinking for a brief period of time, dis-identified as Muslim or disavowed
their faith (c.f. Valentine and Sporton 2009). This accords with the findings of a
study of men aged 16–38 of Pakistani Muslim heritage living in Bradford UK,
which found that Islam was a key aspect of the informants' spiritual, personal and
political lives, and that all defined themselves as Muslim despite following various
religious practices (Alam and Husband 2006). Instead, the informants in this study
who had drunk alcohol regarded drinking by young men within the Pakistani
Muslim community as a temporary phase that was not necessarily incompatible
with their faith. Rather, it was argued that drinking often occurs during transitions
to adulthood but that once young Muslim men marry they pay more heed to
their religious responsibilities and that repentance ensures forgiveness for past
misdemeanours. On marriage, family duty (particularly the importance of not
tarnishing the family's honour) and social/community obligations must outweigh
individuals' personal desires (Yip 2004), and so at this point most men abstain
from consuming alcohol. As such, for these informants generational differences
in attitudes towards and the consumption of, alcohol does not represent a threat
to the Muslim faith because they understand religious and cultural commitment

to unfold over time, and notwithstanding the practices of young people, regard adulthood within the British Muslim Pakistani community to be still embedded in the collective traditions of the faith. For these informants, alcohol consumption represents a process of transition rather than a generational shift in attitudes and behaviour:

> What I've seen a lot of people do grow out of it as soon as they get into their twenties, they do start drinking about sixteen, seventeen years old, and they do very slowly grow out of it, and mainly generally the places they're buying them from is, just buy them from the off-licence and drink them in the parks and like that, don't really get into the habit of going to the pubs or clubs or something like that ...
>
> (Bazid Nazar, Stoke-on-Trent, 25–34, Male, NS-SEC 3)

> The same people age as me you'd find a lot of them say yeah we go out drinking but I don't think you'd find many of them say oh we think it's a good thing to do. I think that the Asian or the Muslim traditions or the reasons why you don't drink will still be deeply upheld...believed in, even though you don't necessarily abide by them at this stage of your life.
>
> (Uddin Masood aged 25–34).

In this respect, the informants argued that drinking by young men is an absent presence in the Pakistani Muslim community because the community knows that it occurs but this behaviour is not publicly acknowledged or managed, indeed it is rarely acknowledged within families either, except between siblings. Some informants claimed that this is because Pakistani Muslim family relations still follow a tradition hierarchical model of parenting, in contrast to the more relational approach adopted in wider British society (Valentine 2004), and are therefore characterized more generally by a less open intergenerational dialogue. In the final section we explore, the implications of Muslim cultures of abstinence in relation to debates about the night-time economy and social cohesion.

Night-time Economy: Impact on Encounters and Social Cohesion

As we discussed in Chapter 1, over the past 20 years urban regeneration programmes in the UK and in many other contemporary western societies have focused on transforming cities through consumption in which hospitality spaces, such as bars, clubs and restaurants, have played a significant role alongside processes of gentrification (e.g. Smith 1996) and the deregulation of licensing (Latham 2003). Stoke-on-Trent's *Community Strategy* for example, promotes the night-time economy as part of its regeneration agenda. Between 1997 and 1999 the capacity of Stoke-on-Trent's licensed premises rose by 242 per cent. Within Stoke-on-Trent's City Centre there are 18 public houses which are licensed to sell alcohol up to 23.00hrs and 28 special hour certificate premises which are licensed to sell alcohol into the early hours, usually until 02.00hrs. There are 13 off-licenses, 26 licensed restaurants and 16 fast food late night refreshment house premises. The combined capacity for the bars and nightclubs during an evening within the City Centre is approximately 25,000 people. In spring 2003 the City Council introduced an on-street alcohol ban for the city centre in response to alcohol related disorder.

In this widespread urban renaissance, exemplified here by Stoke-on-Trent's strategy – the city has been celebrated as a meeting place – a coming together of differences – to build mutual recognition and interdependence (e.g. Laurier and Philo 2006; Iveson 2006; Bell 2007). Alcohol – which anthropological research suggests is, in most times and cultures, a social act which through reciprocity facilitates the development and maintenance of social bonds (SIRC 1998; see also Burns et al. 2002; Putnam 2000) – has been particularly credited with contributing to the creation of civic identities and engendering 'community' (e.g. Chatterton and Hollands 2002 – notwithstanding the highly publicized problems of urban consumers drinking to excess and creating disorder). Latham (2003, 1712), for example, drawing on case study work in Auckland, New Zealand, argues that its contemporary public culture of drinking and eating has created a purpose to sociability and produced the pretext for strangers to meet, so building new solidarities, in this case queering public space. Other studies have acknowledged the role that drinking spaces aimed at women consumers have played in the feminization of urban public space and the creation of new gender relations.

While this research supports Latham's (2003, and Latham and McCormack's 2004) thesis about the generative role of alcohol in producing social relations, the experience of our Pakistani Muslim interviewees is that alcohol does not reconfigure urban relationships for this particular group in positive ways, but rather is producing new unanticipated forms of exclusion. In this sense, our research chimes with a strand of anthropological research which has demonstrated the way that laws, customs and social practices around alcohol are/have been used by societies in a range of cultural and historical contexts to differentiate populations by for example, age, gender, class (e.g. Douglas 1987; Gefou-Madianou 1999) as well as to distinguish between different ethnic groups (e.g. Vaillant's 1983 comparison between Irish and Jewish Americans). Specifically, this research suggests that alcohol structures the use of urban public space in the night-time economy through normative social codes of behaviour predicated on drinking (involving complex rituals of reciprocity and sociality) which implicitly determine whom the place is for and how the space should habitually be occupied and used. Drinking alcohol is seen as what young people and adults in the UK, mainland Europe, North America, Australia and New Zealand 'normally do' (Nairn et al. 2006), and as such heavy drinking circuits (and associated public drunkenness and disorder) are associated with urban centres at night:

> Well drink's everywhere, it doesn't matter where you go, even when you go to snooker halls and that you've got people drinking in there, so its virtually

everywhere. Wherever you go there'll be drinking, drinking will be associated everywhere you go so you just take ... keep myself to myself [edit] Generally amongst Muslims to see drink is hurtful you know.

(Harun Rana, Stoke-on-Trent, 25–34, Male, NS-SEC 3)

While non-alcoholic drinks are also available in many venues in the night-time economy, Muslims commonly chose not to enter these spaces because they are uncomfortable and feel 'out of place' (Cresswell 1996) in spaces associated with alcohol, as well as risking their own and their family's reputation by being associated with drinking places. Our informants generally described self-excluding themselves from public places, or events where alcohol is involved referring to these as sites of corruption, and as 'dirty' or 'illegal' (under Islamic law) spaces. In this sense, interviewees described spaces where alcohol was served as potentially having the affect of 'contaminating' or defiling them:

[Describing people drunk in the city centre] I think it's downright disgusting cos they're actually making a mockery of themselves they've got no respect for themselves really I mean to me it's all alien and believe it or not I really stop myself now from going out of anything like that, it's the type of environment, I'd rather not go into it [edit] It's respect for yourself, respect for your religion, respect for culture. It's just something you don't want to go into, just something you don't want to get exposed into, simple facts is that if you cross that bridge then there's no boundaries there [edit] I do ... socializing during the day now as opposed to the evenings cos simple fact like I said...the whole drinking and smoking aspect and then the way people act and react towards you or other people when their bodies are intoxicated so I'd just rather not go there.

(Zahra Mahomed, Stoke-on-Trent, 45–54, Female, NS-SEC 7)

You get a few comments at work when people say, I think when we used to finish at work for say the holidays like Christmas and so on and people used to say oh are you coming down the pub and so on after work, and I'd say 'oh no I don't drink'. [Then mimics his colleagues' response] 'What, you don't drink, have you got a life?' So obviously that shows what they think of drinking. Anyway, I say 'yeah, fine thanks, yeah I have a good life' actually but I don't drink, simple as that...

(Bazid Nazar, Stoke-on-Trent, 25–34, Male, NS-SEC 3)

I wouldn't be in an environment where there's alcohol at all. [Interviewer do you ever go to the town centre?] Not at night, during the day only for shopping, for socialising no, stay away from the place, too much corruption.

(Afzul Mohammed, Stoke-on-Trent, 45–54, Male, NS-SEC 4)

Other research with individuals who are non-drinkers (Nairn et al. 2006), though not on the grounds of religious belief, has found that some attempt to 'pass' by pretending that they are drinking alcohol (e.g. by consuming clear liquids that are easily mistaken for drinks such as vodka) or pretending they are drunk in order to participate in their social networks: to be 'in place'. This tactic of invisibility however, is less possible for our interviewees because as Pakistani Muslims they are representatives of a religion that abstains from alcohol and so they would be more, not less, noticeable if they appeared to 'drink' in public. Moreover, by passing as if they were drinking in a public space the Pakistani Muslim interviewees would risk word of this 'behaviour' reaching their Muslim community with all the damage to their familial honor that this would entail (Bradby 2007). Not surprisingly, as we outlined in the section above, Pakistani Muslims who drink tend to do so in marginal spaces rather than in the mainstream night-time economy. In this way, the emphasis on alcohol in the night-time economy has the effect of filtering access to public space and therefore excluding the Muslim population from the opportunity to engage in urban conviviality with all the possibilities for the type of encounters it offers which are credited with facilitating good relations between diverse social groups.

Rather, Pakistani Muslim young people in particular, create their own oppositional leisure spaces (such as small independent businesses, cafes, canteens and other types of social spaces) without alcohol which helps them to maintain their own faith value systems and strengthen their own religious commitments and identities, although accounts of these spaces are largely missing from discussions of the night-time economy. In Stoke-on-Trent these spaces are commonly located in specific neighbourhood communities rather than the city centre and are not frequented by white majority customers (i.e. they should not be confused with restaurants and cafes providing Pakistani and South Indian food in the mainstream night-time economy). Through such processes alcohol has agency, effectively contributing to the social segregation of the Muslim population from white majority night-time economy leisure spaces. In other words, this 'new' form of exclusion, like the queer space identified by Latham (2003) in Auckland, New Zealand, represents a transformation of space that is emergent in nature, that is, it is the outcome of the unforeseen affective power of alcohol rather than of intentional decision-making or planning by local authorities or commercial investors (c.f. Latham and McCormack 2004). In this sense, this chapter offers further evidence to support the argument that the process of contemporary urban renaissance, evident in many western cities, is actually threatening the diversity of urban social life because of its orientation towards certain types of mainstream consumer and patterns of consumption (e.g. Davis 1991; Zukin 1995; Smith 1996; Fyfe and Bannister 1996; Mitchell 1997; Valentine 1996) and its failure to acknowledge alternative consumers and the spaces they create and inhabit. As Phillips et al. (2006) has argued in relation to the residential segregation of the British Asian population, such patterns are often represented as 'choice' when in fact they are a product, at least in part, of wider exclusionary processes.

Conclusion

In this chapter we have explored the generative role of alcohol in producing social relations, demonstrating the agency of alcohol in contributing to the social segregation of the Muslim population from night-time economy leisure spaces. In particular, we have highlighted how the 'normalization' of consuming alcohol in UK culture shapes expectations about the use of (and implicitly also access to) public space and spatial norms within the mainstream night-time economy. Indeed, Talbot (2007, 86) has described the role of licensed premises as an economic driver of UK mainstream urban night-time economies and the liberalization of licensing laws as representing a 'loosening of moral boundaries characteristic of neo-liberalism' in which notions of commercial or consumer viability have been allowed to determine, in effect, what is socially acceptable in public. As such we would argue it is time to reflect on some of the unintentional consequences of this laissez-faire approach to the night-time economy and to frame this within a broader debate about issues of national cultural identity, morality and social cohesion. Notably, our findings suggest that there is a need for more intentional planning and regulation of urban night-time economies to recognize the diverse ways that alcohol is absent and present in the city and the diverse nature of hospitality spaces that exist within different community spaces in order to support the development of a wider range of mainstream leisure spaces that are less predicated on the consumption of alcohol. This might facilitate access to opportunities for social groups such as Muslims (but also other faith groups, as well as other social groupings such as the young, old) who abstain from alcohol to participate in mainstream urban social life. In taking such an approach, it might be possible to create more spaces for meaningful encounters between different social groups that might otherwise not have many opportunities for social contact and thus facilitate the development of good relations (Valentine 2008).

At the same time our research also highlights the need for alcohol support services (both non governmental organizations and charities such as Alcohol Concern, Alcoholics Anonymous) as well as government departments with responsibility for alcohol harm reduction strategies to target communities with cultures of abstention in order to reach 'hidden' levels of problem drinking. The Cochrane and Bal (1990) study, cited above, found that while Asian men were prepared to turn to family members or to a doctor/hospital for help with alcohol problems, they were significantly less likely to seek out alternative sources of help (e.g. voluntary organizations or support groups such as Alcoholic Anonymous) than informants from the white majority population. For example, a substance abuse agency in Bradford, with a high minority ethnic (and faith) population, found only 1 per cent of its service users were non-white compared to 20 per cent of the local population. It identified barriers to potential users from minority ethnic communities accessing its services as including: a lack of awareness of the existence of the service; an assumption that it would be white-run and catering for white-clients (based on the potential service users' experiences of other health and welfare services in the area) where service users from minority ethnic communities may encounter racism or a lack of cultural sensitivity; language barriers; and also concerns about appearing to corroborate negative stereotypes of minority communities by identifying themselves as having a problem (Harrison et al. 1996). Such findings have led to calls for the development of appropriate specialist services to reach minority ethnic and faith communities. However, there is also a risk that targeting minority ethnic groups in this way may exacerbate the marginalization of mainstream service provision for these groups. Moreover, the evidence of this research is that Muslim clients may prefer speaking to a non-Muslim counsellor because of fears that their confidentiality might not be maintained in close-knit local Asian communities if services were to be staffed by their own community members (see also Patel 1993; Harrison et al. 1996). Rather, several commentators have suggested that the solution instead is to recruit and train generic mainstream service providers more appropriately, and to conduct appropriate community outreach work to discover the needs of communities that traditionally abstain from alcohol in order to build relations of trust (e.g. Ahmed 1989; Patel 1993; McKeigue and Karmi 1993).

Chapter 6
Generations

In most contemporary societies in the global north there is growing concern about rising levels of alcohol consumption, particularly by young people, even in countries, such as France and Italy, which have previously been assumed to have 'sensible' drinking cultures (Wright 1999; Järvinen and Room 2007). However, while alcohol research has focused on issues such as the transmission of parents alcohol related behaviour to their children's drinking patterns (Yu 2004; Lieb 2002; Conway et al. 2003), and considered the influence of family life on young people's attitudes towards drinking (Lowe et al. 1993; Shucksmith et al. 1997; Tlusty 2004; Marquis 2004; Bogenschneider et al. 1998) research agendas to date have failed to look at generational influences relating to alcohol, drinking and drunkenness beyond the parent/child relationship. Indeed, recent popular and policy debates about UK drinking cultures – particularly the emergence of binge drinking by young people in Southern Europe have hinted at a shift in generational attitudes towards alcohol, as well as patterns of consumption. Previous intergenerational studies of work and care have found that in particular historical periods different normativities develop, reflecting both social and economic conditions (Brannen et al. 2004). Given post-war shifts in the nature and type of alcohol products on the market, price, availability (i.e. growth in off-trade sales) and the more recent liberalization of licensing laws in the UK it is reasonable to anticipate that different cohorts may have developed different normativities in relation to drinking. In this chapter we discuss the evidence as to whether these assumptions in relation to alcohol are proven, and if so how patterns of drinking have changed, and what may have been the drivers for any social transformations in attitudes and practices between different generations.

My Generation: Remembered Attitudes Towards, and Consumption of Alcohol

Generation is a fuzzy term that is used in diverse ways by different groups of scholars. Kinship studies (e.g. Pilcher 1995) use the term 'generation' to describe lineage from child, to parent, to grandparent which Arber and Attias Donfut (2000, 2) suggest might be more accurately be described as *'family generations'*. Other scholars use generation to describe people of a similar age who were born at the same time in history: *'cohort generations'*. In this sense, what is normative for each cohort generation is different and each cohort may therefore behave in ways that were uncommon or even unthinkable to previous generations (Brannen et al. 2004). In a seminal essay the sociologist Mannheim (1952) linked the formation of generations to social change (sometimes referred to as 'historical generations'). He argued that people who share a particular significant experience (e.g. major social upheavals such as the Great Depression, a war, a period of rapid social change such as the 1960s etc.) develop a shared sense of social or political consciousness and vision of the world. Attias-Donfut (1988) has argued that this notion of historical generation is perhaps over valorized because generations are continually evolving regardless of whether they experience major social upheaval or live through more subtle social change; and that historical generation is often a product of a social imaginary that instantiates a particular moment as a collective memory of society. In this chapter, we draw on generation in two of these ways. First, our informants were recruited as family generations (following the male line in some families, and the female line in others). Second, for the purposes of analysis we banded the informants into three cohort generations. These we refer to in the chapter for convenience as the 'older generation': those aged over 65 (i.e. of retirement age); the 'mid-generation', aged between 35–54; and the 'youth generation' aged 18 to 24 (i.e. young adulthood: this age range is commonly defined as 'youth' in social studies of childhood).

The older generation of the majority population is the group which grew up in a historical period when there was significant social prohibition on alcohol consumption (they were teenagers in the 1950s). There was little, if any alcohol kept or consumed at home (except perhaps sherry at Christmas), and drinking in public space during the period of their youth was generally a male pursuit. While the interviewees cannot recall specific parental discussion about, or rules in relation to, alcohol consumption they were aware that there were unspoken expectations which meant that they were inhibited from openly drinking underage in front of their parents. Nonetheless, all the men recalled 'dabbling' in drink without their parents' knowledge. Men commonly recalled the age of their first drink at around 15–16, and women later. Underage drinking by young men – particularly in 'working-class' and rural areas – when accompanied by fathers or another male relative was sometimes sanctioned within community spaces like the pub. Indeed, the pub was an important social space as much for meeting, talking, playing dominos and so on, as for drinking. It was also a space that had implicit expectations of behaviour which were informally policed:

> Dale: My father from when I was a small child you know…he used to go to pub, especially Sunday dinner, and he…used to be out…he stopped about half past two, three, whatever you know.
>
> Interviewer: And would he ever drink at home as well?

Dale: Never had any, any drink at home [edit] up the road there's a little pub, always seemed to be empty and we used to go in and I was about 15. And I think he [the landlord] was desperate because he was getting no customers and there was always about two or three halves [half pints of beer] at that time like, we were singing and doing two or three halves. I suppose that was the first time I'd say I had any drink you know.

(Dale Harper, Stoke-on-Trent, 65+, Male, NS-SEC 3)

I used to go down to the pub and say he'd [his father] got you a half [half pint of beer] there and … I went down one night with a … big … collar and he pulled me on one side and he'd got a couple of his mates there. And he said don't come down here, don't come down here like that, he said. Collar and tie. This was a bloody Thursday night this was, half past ten, yeah, and I never, I didn't argue with him, I respected what he said.

(Carl Allan, Stoke-on-Trent, 65+, Male, NS-SEC 4)

However, women's drinking was still considered to be socially unacceptable and was much less visible in public space than men's drinking. Indeed, for women leaving home commonly offered the first freedom to drink. Like, the male interviewees, women also recalled that 'going out' or having a drink was motivated by a desire to be sociable or have fun, not by the alcohol itself or the pursuit of drunkenness. Interviewees from this generation suggested that it was rare to see public displays of drunkenness; indeed in Eden village dances were still commonly alcohol free. The most common drink for young men was beer and for young women drinks like Cherry B:

You didn't see a lot of drunkenness … In our young days and our grown up days, very, very occasionally saw anybody drunk … No, it was a totally different atmosphere. Totally [edit] When I was young there was never a woman in a pub. It just didn't happen … you'd get in the pubs five or six elderly gentlemen having a pint and smoking pipes and that was about it … I should think I would be 20 at least I would imagine before I ever saw women drinking slightly.

(Colin Bellis, Eden, 65+, Male, NS-SEC 3)

None of the older generation Pakistani Muslim interviewees had ever drunk alcohol because it is forbidden by Islam. This culture of abstinence is regulated by close-knit family and community socials network which produce strong expectations of integration and conformity to shared values, such as abstinence (Dwyer 1999; see Chapter 5). This interviewee described how when he was working in a factory he was even careful to avoid drinking soft drinks like colas in case his workmates spiked them with alcohol:

It is totally forbidden in Islam and in all my life I have never drank, never, never in my life. I've never drank in my life. Some Muslims do drink but it's forbidden,

Muslims should never drink in their life … it is against Islam … a person who
reads, who submits himself to Allah should not drink and a person that drinks all
he does is fight with his family … [Recalling his youth] I never went out with
my friends, I used to go down to the Mosque do my prayers, remember Allah. I
never went to pubs with my friends, I went to the Mosque I came home.

(Husnan Ibadulla, Stoke-on-Trent, 65+, Male, NS-SEC 7)

A significant change in attitudes towards, and practices of, alcohol consumption
in public space (though not private space) is evident in the mid generation of
the majority population's accounts of their own childhoods/youth (in the mid/late
1970s to 1980s). The mid generation recall that alcohol played an important role in
their parents' lives. Amongst the middle-class respondents most of them remember
a drinks cabinet at home, that alcohol was evident when their parents would
entertain friends for dinner parties while they and their siblings were banished
upstairs, and that drink driving was more socially acceptable than today (indeed
some of the interviewees recalled drinking driving themselves in their youth).
Among the interviewees from 'working-class' backgrounds alcohol consumption
was still more strongly associated with public drinking and was particularly
something that fathers did at the pub.

For this generation, most of the majority population were introduced to,
or allowed to experiment with, alcohol at Christmas or other special family
occasions. Fifteen or 16 were, for this generation of both men and women much
like the older male generation, the ages at which they first started independently
to drink. This generation also described how they drank underage without their
parents' knowledge in both commercial venues (such as pubs) and out of bottles
and cans in informal public spaces (such as with friends in church yards, in the
park, at youth clubs and so on). This involved trying to 'pass' as older in pubs,
and obtaining alcohol from siblings or from the family home to drink in informal
public spaces with friends. These practices were key elements of joining and
participating in different local drinking cultures, and involved negotiating or
asserting this membership with relatives. The motivation to drink was therefore
still sociality as well as a desire belong or fit in:

Interviewer: What were your first experiences [of drinking?]

Gary: Just in the village pub at 16 I think I started going in there…we used to
drink cider, bottles of Bulmer's cider, I think if I remember rightly … I also
remember yes, friend of mine, his father's supply … I'd have a few bottles
of that [Edit – referring to when he was a few years older] We'd go to Penrith
[the nearest town] different places, different nights … just to pubs, not clubs or
anything … And an odd nightclub in Carlisle we used to go there every Sunday
… they had a live group every Sunday night [Edit] when I was their age [his
children's age] we did tend to drink and drive a bit … very, very, very rarely you
ever see any 17, 18, 19 year olds in the village [now] drinking and driving … it's

advertised a bit better now isn't it [dangers of drink driving]? Like all the, there's more police around ... When I was younger I mean if you saw a policeman in the village once a month you were, you just didn't see anyone.

(Gary Bellis, Eden, 45–54, Male, NS-SEC 3)

Donna: I was about 17 [when she started drinking]. We were not allowed to go to the pub but we would go, that's when I would go when I was about 17 ... I wasn't of age ... we would go in and buy it [lager] ourselves.

Interviewer: Did the people know that you were under age?

Donna: They must have done. Definitely one would know that we were underage and they would serve us ... To begin with not very much and then it progressed that we would drink more ... Not to be drunk, that we didn't know what we were doing, definitely not, but to be half way I think ... it was cool ... and I think that's why I drank. I didn't drink because I particularly liked it, I liked the feeling and it was you know everybody did it.

(Donna Kirkland, Eden, 35–44, Male, NS-SEC 5)

The most common first drinks recalled were lager, beer/ales and cider. While men continued to drink lager or beer/ales throughout their youth, women described progressing to drinking spirits with sweet mixers, such as Bacardi and coke and brandy and Babycham. Sometimes the interviewees had been caught out drinking by their parents, several recalled experiences of getting very drunk and then being sick or passing out when they got home. As Jane Cox remembers:

Jane: The only thing I remember is when I would come in ... extremely pissed. And my Dad kind of telling me how stupid I was or something but I don't, yeah, desperately trying to get him to shut up because I was just about ... be sick [laughs] ... I remember my sister coming in drunk ... My sister's about 7 years older than me, so I would have been quite little ... And my Mum giving her salt water and making her sick, I can remember. So I guess there was a very clear message from them around not drinking.

Interviewer: so you mentioned coming in drunk one night, what would your first experiences of drinking be?

Jane: I would think that drinking with mates and stuff ... and we'd like use the park a lot, evenings, had a lot of, lots of kind of beer and cider and stuff. And so memories of me drinking would be I suppose, I think probably cider and stuff, although I do remember, I've never really liked lager or beer but I remember trying that, cans and stuff ... And there used to be pubs around there who obviously were very careful about who they would serve [sarcastically], and so again you'd be able to go in and be able to get served in there. And I

remember sometimes that would be quite tricky [because they were underage]
but other times absolutely fine about it.

(Jane Cox, Stoke-on-Trent-on-Trent, 45–54, Female, NS-SEC 2)

As this type of drinking was typically done without parents' knowledge and in
many cases against family 'rules', these misdemeanours often resulted in a stern
telling off (as some of the above quotes indicate), several of the interviewees also
recalled that their parents acknowledged in reprimanding them that – 'you have
learnt your lesson now'.

While there is evidence therefore of change between the older and mid
generations' amongst the majority population interviewees, this pattern was not
evident within the sample of Muslim Pakistani families because their religious
belief and consequently its associated culture of abstinence has remained
largely consistent across the generations. Only one mid generation interviewee
admitted to drinking alcohol. He consumes a moderate amount (15–21 units per
week), mainly spirits, in city centre pubs (i.e. not within his own neighbourhood
community where he may be seen) with non-Muslim friends to be sociable, and
relax. However, he never drinks at home and conceals his drinking from his wife,
children and extended family because of their shared religious belief. Rather, the
majority of the Pakistani Muslim informants described the difficulties they have
experienced avoiding alcohol in a public culture where it is readily available:

> I remember I was at Pizza Hut with some friends...I was sitting there having
> something to eat, we are there enjoying ourselves, having a great time and what
> not, all of a sudden … one of the waiters basically brings out a bottle of wine
> and I'm sitting there very, very calmly yet still in shock but not trying to make it
> obvious at the fact … for the first time, I know it's going to sound a bit sad, for
> the first time I've actually been that close to a bottle of alcohol, seeing it open,
> being poured into people's glasses … it was very, very shocking.
>
> (Zahra Mahomed, Stoke-on-Trent, 45–54, Female, NS-SEC 6)

The current 'youth generation' from majority population families largely recall
being introduced to alcohol at a young age within a familial context and describe
a more relaxed attitude from their parents towards their experiments with alcohol
than the mid and older generations. Several interviewees recounted examples
of when their parents or friends parents would allow them to consume alcohol
underage with their friends in the home either before, or instead of going out.
In these instances, young people thought their drinking was supported by their
parents in order to encourage them to stay in the safe space of the home, rather
than going out with friends (see Chapter 3). In some cases within Eden parents also
gave underage young people alcohol to drink in informal spaces outside the home
with their friends, reflecting the role of alcohol in rural communities where there
are limited alternative social and leisure opportunities for young people (Ward
1990; Philo 1992). This generation also describe experiences of going to pubs

with their parents – like the older generation -- in which they were also sometimes provided with socially sanctioned underage access to alcohol (cf. Leyshon 2007). Nonetheless, despite this more open atmosphere some young people also described patterns of illicit drinking without their parents' knowledge in both informal spaces and commercial venues that bear strong echoes of the mid generation's accounts of drinking in parks, beaches and so on:

> ... the pub, I was like 16 and they used to let you, if I was with Dad they used to let us have a drink of something, on a night, just bottles again of your weak lager.
>
> (Ellie Bellis, Eden, 18–24, Female, NS-SEC 3)

> I used to go around like to ... the disco until 11 o'clock or something. And that would just be like older people there and they were drinking. And like we used to get our hands on like vodka and stuff and just. Yeah, well we didn't know anything really, we didn't, it was just the sort of, because it was like, we were getting to that age where it was too boring for us.
>
> (Melissa Worthington, Eden, 18–24, Female, NS-SEC 2)

> I suppose my real memory ... I suppose was at school when I was about 15 and, and all my friends sort of going out and buying cider and drinking it outside school ... you know sort of hanging around in groups and sort of trying to find somebody to go in and buy cheap drinks ... It would just be like sort of very sociable, just chatting with friends and you know, drinking.
>
> (Gail Cox, Stoke-on-Trent, 18–24, Female, NS-SEC 2)

This generation's preferred drink however, is vodka, although young women also drink wine, alcopops and spirits with sweet mixers such as Archers and lemonade. These interviewees also described strong peer pressure to drink, and particularly for young women to keep up with the pace of their male counterparts' drinking. Their main motivation for drinking is to get drunk because in the words of one informant 'you can't have fun unless you are off your head'. Here, alcohol was described as crucial in order to give young people the confidence to flirt with the opposite sex and to be relaxed enough to be considered 'fun' by their friends.

Amongst the Pakistani Muslim youth generation there was significant evidence of drinking amongst young men (see Chapter 5). From the interviewees' accounts of their own, or observations of their peers' behaviour, a common pattern appears to be that young men start drinking in their mid to late teens. The main motivation mirrors that of majority informants: a desire to be sociable and to fit in with peer groups as well as to loose their inhibitions and in particular gain confidence with women. Yet, because of the social prohibition about drinking within the Muslim community most of this consumption takes place in marginal public spaces (parks, bus shelters and so on) – and never at home – because young drinkers want to avoid the risk of being seen drinking by other Muslims and therefore bringing shame on both themselves and their family (although some informants did describe risking going to public venues in parts of the city not frequented by the Pakistani community). Drinking by women however is much more strongly prohibited and policed by families and the wider Pakistani Muslim community than that by young men. This mirrors the more general regulation of women's bodies and identities, which is facilitated by the close-knit nature of family and social life within British Muslim communities (Dwyer 1999; Bradby 2007). The costs of transgressing community 'norms' are also potentially more severe for women. However, unlike, the older and mid generation in the Pakistani Muslim community, the youth generation is willing to tolerate other people drinking in their presence or to be in venues where alcohol is served even if they themselves chose to abstain from alcohol on the grounds of their religious belief. One young woman even described allowing guests who visit her house to bring and consume their own alcohol in her home even though she does not drink on the grounds of her religion:

> The attitude's the same [across the generations of his family] towards that [drinking alcohol], you shouldn't drink, it's wrong to drink and so the attitude's the same. Maybe in my family I'm more tolerable to seeing other people drink than my father or my grandfather would be. But that's just because my father lived in Pakistan for, until he was 12, 13 years old, and his father worked as soon as they arrived into England. Now because I've grown up and been able to go to college and now I'm at university I've seen the drink culture more and more often so I'm more tolerable with people than maybe my father and me grandfather would be and me mother [edit] I'll go out with my friends, they'll be drinking but I won't be drinking, I'll have some Red Bulls, some coke etc … and then we'll go home and I'll drive home at the end of the night because I'll be the sober one out of the lot of us.
>
> (Shadaf Ibadulla, Stoke-on-Trent, 18–24, Female, NS-SEC 7)

Continuities and Discontinuities in Drinking Practices Across the Generations

What is striking about the patterns of alcohol consumption described by each majority cohort generation in the previous section is that the most significant differences occurred between the older and mid generations, rather than between the mid and young generations. It was between the older and mid generations that drinking became a more widespread leisure practice; alcohol became commonplace within the home; the type and availability of products changed, and women's drinking increased, becoming more visible in public space. Amongst the Pakistani Muslim informants change is more evident between the mid and youth generations where there is more evidence of experimentation with alcohol by young men (albeit usually as a temporary phase).

There are some notable continuities however between the drinking patterns of young people in the latter two generations of the majority population. Both the older and mid generation started drinking underage when they were aged about 15 to 17 years old in marginal public spaces (such as parks, the streets, outside youth clubs), as well as in pubs with alcohol bought by those who could 'pass' as older than their age or supplied by friends/relatives. Both groups also moved to drinking regularly in pubs, bars and clubs once they were over 18. In this sense, there is little evidence that wider social changes over the last 30 years such as the liberalization of drinking hours and the growth in the availability of alcohol at home as a result of off-trade retail sales have particularly affected young people's age of first drink or early patterns of consumption.

However, what is significant is the different *type of products* that young majority people in each cohort generation have consumed. Whereas the older and mid generation interviewees began their drinking careers with lager, beer and cider – not moving onto spirits until they were into adulthood; the youth generation started underage with vodka and other types of shots as well as alcopops. As such, the youth generation are actually consuming significantly more units of alcohol than both the other generations, despite broadly following the same pattern of drinking activities as the mid generation. This is supported by the evidence of a review which synthesized the findings from a number of large national cross-sectional surveys. It found that contemporary young people are drinking twice what they were in 1990 (Smith and Foxcroft 2009).

A second key difference between the mid and youth generations is the *motivation to drink*. The youth generation describe deliberately going out to get drunk (what Measham 2006 has labelled 'determined drunkenness'), whereas the mid and the older generations do not recall that such an explicit intentional motive lay behind their patterns of consumption. Rather, the mid generation described how they would go out to meet friends or to have a drink which sometimes led to drinking games, excess consumption, drunkenness and so on but this was not necessarily the objective before the night began. While alcohol was an important means of joining in or participating in social networks, none of the mid generation interviewees recalled peer pressure during their youth to drink to excess. For this generation alcohol was remembered as a contributing factor, but not essential to 'having a good time'.

In contrast, the youth generation regard alcohol itself as crucial to a 'good night'. This generation feel strong pressure from their friends to 'be fun' and 'to have a good time'. Such peer pressure often takes the form of teasing or name-calling (especially accusations of being boring or unsociable) and requests to join in (and therefore to demonstrate they are 'fun') which not only play on individuals' emotional insecurities about their own identities but also provoke guilt about letting the group down, or spoiling the night out for others through their non-conformity (cf. studies of the experience of non-drinkers e.g. Nairn et al. 2006). This pressure is mobilized through an emphasis on round buying and drinking games which increase the speed of a group's drinking and make it difficult for individuals to drink in a different way to that established as the group pattern. Many young people lack self-confidence – which in part reflects the pressures they are under to manage their own biographies (with all the associated choices and risks this involves) in the context of individualization (Beck and Beck-Gernsheim 2002). Their accounts demonstrate how alcohol has agency giving them confidence and enabling them to participate in such pressurized peer social networks by helping them to relax, loose their inhibitions and 'to be fun' replicating the evidence of other studies (e.g. Chatterton and Hollands 2002; Hubbard 2005) that have shown how alcohol heightens affective intensities in a variety of ways:

> When I go out, I go out to get drunk…after you know, you have actually got a few drinks down you, you feel it and you think it feels good because you know you're more confident.
>
> (Melissa Worthington, Eden, 18–24, Female, NS-SEC 2)

> Interviewer: [in response to his description of underage drinking]: So what were you drinking when you were 16 and going out?
>
> Peter: Pretty much anything and everything that I could get my hands on that would get me drunk I think…I was drinking quite a bit of vodka I think because it was going to get me drunk quicker as well … to get, to get plastered.
>
> (Peter Kirkland, Eden, 18–24, Male, NS-SEC 5)

> what worries me is that they go out to get drunk … [comparing her own drinking in her youth to that of her son and daughter] That's what they do, they don't go out to drink socially and then end up drunk, that's the main cause to go out … so that does worry me and I do think they drink such a lot, this binge drinking … It's not a little amount, it's every weekend and it's excess isn't it … it's definitely more than when we were young, definitely is.
>
> (Donna Kirkland, Eden, 35–44, Female NS-SEC 5)

Young men in particular, described the importance of alcohol in facilitating them to talk to and flirt with young women; as well as the competitive nature of masculine drinking cultures in both rural and urban public spaces (see also Kraack and Kenway 2002; Leyshon 2005; Nayak 2003). While there is growing evidence that young women's drinking habits are increasingly similar to young men's (Wright 1999) our participant observation found that young men commonly drink more quickly than young women, whereas young women wait for last person in a round to finish a drink before the next round is purchased, young men will buy consecutive rounds regards of the groups' actual consumption so that the slower drinkers may accumulate two or three drinks. Indeed, some of the young women interviewed also observed the gendered nature of peer pressure, describing how their female friends would look after each other on a 'night out'; whereas their male counterparts would deliberately try to get each other drunk.

Women's patterns of alcohol consumption have significantly increased from one generation to the next (as the above accounts demonstrate) as a result of women's changing position in the labour market and the emergence of 'new femininities' which has seen young and professional women specifically targeted by the alcohol and nightlife industry in terms of the development of new products and new types of venue (Chatterton and Holland 2002; Plant and Plant 2006). A research review which synthesized the findings of seven large national surveys over the last 20–30 years found a significant increase in drinking by women and that the gender gap between men and women's drinking behaviours is narrowing (Smith and Foxcroft 2009). Yet, moral attitudes to women's drinking in public space have not quite kept pace with this social change: women drinkers still face more opprobrium than their male counterparts (Plant 1997; Day et al. 2004). While there is greater recognition of women's right to drink and of their visibility in public drinking venues; nonetheless both male and female interviewees in our study were critical of women who are visibly drunk in public space. This moral hangover in terms of social attitudes reflects the persistence of traditional gendered (and classed) expectations of 'respectability': that although women may drink in public they are expected to retain self-control and manage their performance of the self when doing so. Failure to do so is to evoke historical sexual discourses about women in public space as 'loose', making themselves vulnerable to male violence, inadequate mothers, invading male domains and so on. These gendered moralities are particular to both age and geographical location:

> When I was younger I never saw any drunken females ... never. They may have just had as I say an egg flip or two, might have been a bit giggly ... but the last 15 years ... the girls, some of them are 17, 19, maybe younger ... and they can knock it back you know. I don't think it's impressive. I don't think it's that impressive ... yeah, I've never seen, up until a few years ago, I've never seen that ... Well it's sad in a way really, you know I'm all for having a good time but it's the girls ... I mean lads are lads.
>
> (Carl Allan, Stoke-on-Trent, 65+, Male, NS-SEC 4)

> It's really acceptable thing for young men to go out and get drunk, that's still the case ... I think you know it's great, you know, that's fine, when it's a young woman who's really drunk, then it's horrible. I think there's a difference there, definitely ... I think it's disgusting, I really do.
>
> (Gail Cox, Stoke-on-Trent, 18–24, Female, NS-SEC 2)

A final significant difference between the three generations of majority interviewees relates to the *accessibility of alcohol in the home* and the concomitant *attitude of parents* towards how young people should be introduced to the practice of drinking. As the accounts in the above section indicate the presence of alcohol in the home has increased from one generation to the next (from a rare treat at Christmas amongst the older generation through to an ever present in the homes of the youth generation – see Chapter 3). The last decade has witnessed an increase in off-trade sales of alcohol in the UK (e.g. through supermarkets, off-licenses and other forms of retailing) as a result of the competitive use of pricing and promotions by retailers. According to a review by Smith and Foxcroft (2009) alcohol is 65 per cent more affordable now than in 1980 and accounts for only 5.2 per cent of household spending compared to 7.5 per cent in 1980 (Office for National Statistic 2007). Most notably, the price of wine has fallen relative to average earnings (Mintel 2005). As a result of its greater affordability many of our middle-class interviewees described how their home consumption of wine has increased. An estimated 80 plus per cent of all wine sold is now through the off-trade (Mintel 2005). As such, it is perhaps not surprising that recent Mintel research (2003) showed that 46 per cent of British adults consume most of their alcohol at home compared with 31 per cent in France and 23 per cent in Spain. Many of our interviewees not only keep alcohol at home for their own consumption but also stock a range of other drinks so that they can offer appropriate hospitality to family and friends. Indeed, some non-drinkers even have alcohol at home to offer visitors (see Chapter 3):

> I mean you can … it's availability … you can go to the supermarket and buy a bottle of whisky, a bottle of, tins of lager, tins of beer. Whereas [in the past] you'd have to go especially to an off-licence or go to the pub then, where[as] now if you go out shopping it's just convenient you can buy it can't you? ... And it's cheaper … if you buy a bottle of wine for two or three quid, cheap whisky for a tenner … I mean when I was younger brandy and whisky used to be pricey … if you were drinking a shot then it was twice the amount of beer … Where now you can go and buy a bottle in the supermarket for ten pounds … spirits are definitely much cheaper than they used to be.
>
> (Gary Bellis, Eden, 45–54, Male, NS-SEC 3)

This intergenerational domestication of alcohol is potentially significant because some studies have shown that the availability of alcohol at home is related to higher levels of drinking amongst young people (van Zundert et al. 2006). Likewise, previous research indicates that the most likely place where children obtain alcohol from is their own home or their friends' homes (Yu et al. 1997). More broadly, it is well established in the alcohol studies literature that the family is a major influence on the development of the drinking careers of young people in relation to both drinking habits and attitudes to drinking (e.g. Raskin White et al. 1991; Plant 2001). Parents directly influence young people through modelling and reinforcing particular practices (Yu et al. 1997).

Mothers and fathers also potentially influence young people's attitude towards and practices of consumption through the parenting practices in terms of the boundaries they set about at what age, when and where it is appropriate for young people to have access to alcohol and how they communicate about drinking related issues. Indeed, there has been a notable shift in parenting ideologies across each generation. This is because the circumstances in which people are raising families, and in this case making choices about alcohol consumption, has changed so that each generation builds its own view of how to parent in relation to alcohol according to its own particular social context. This is both an *intra-familial* process in that parents have to work out for themselves what is the 'right' thing to do; and an *extra familial* process in which wider public social 'norms' are established and contested (e.g. media, national policy recommendations, local parenting cultures etc.). Through such processes contemporary majority parents are approaching the issue of alcohol in ways that were unthinkable amongst previous generations.

The generational accounts of the majority interviewees in the above section demonstrate the emergence and then relaxation of rules about drinking across the three generations, combined with an increase in communication about alcohol between the mid and young generation. This reflects a broader trend in terms of the changing nature of intergenerational relations. Traditionally, parents have had 'natural' authority over children because of their superior size, strength, age and command of material resources. This authority has been sustained through laws and everyday norms about the appropriate behaviour of adults and children (Jamieson and Toynbee 1989). The older generation recall that because alcohol was rarely present in the home and alcohol was readily available in public space their parents did not have cause to establish specific rules or boundaries in relation to alcohol. Rather there were strong, unspoken extra familial and intra familial expectations about appropriate behaviour which meant that young people were inhibited from openly drinking underage in front of their parents and there was little or no communication about alcohol. For the mid generation, an increasingly liberal approach to alcohol in society, including the emergence of domestic cultures of consumption, meant that their parents laid down strict boundaries in relation to young people's drinking. When these were inevitably broken the mid generation recall being severely reprimanded and receiving little sympathy from their parents when they suffered the ill-effects of experimenting with drink. However, the subsequent growth of processes of individualization has produced a significant change in contemporary adults' attitudes to parenting. Rather than laying down the law with their children parents are now more willing to invite discussion and to negotiate rules and boundaries in the pursuit of closer, less hierarchical relationships with their offspring, with the consequence that there is greater autonomy between the generations and some of adults' 'natural' authority is being eroded (Wyness 1997; Gullestad and Segalen 1997; Beck and Beck-Gernsheim 2002). This extra-familial shift in the emphasis of parenting between cohort generations – from disciplining young people to enabling their expressivity – has produced a marked change in the ways that attitudes and practices about alcohol are transmitted in intra-familial contexts between family generations.

Notably, the mid generation interviewees described a reluctance to assert a hierarchical – 'do as I say but not as I did' – approach to their own children's alcohol consumption. In a contemporary context, where alcohol consumption is constituted as a normal part of everyday life, and excess consumption is seen as a normal and inevitable part of growing up, most contemporary parents of young people (the mid generation) accept that children will drink and were concerned instead to introduce their offspring to alcohol in a family setting (e.g. at meal times) in order to encourage sensible drinking as alcohol becomes more readily available to them in their later teenage years and beyond: an approach which is more normative in countries such as Portugal and Spain (Plant and Miller 2007). Mid generation parents were also aware of the need to avoid alienating young people by being too strict because of a fear that their children might rebel against their rules, drinking in secret, outdoors or in public venues away from the home and thus increasing their vulnerability to alcohol related harms (as they themselves had done as young people). Although, it is worth observing that a survey by Plant and Miller (2007) of 2023 students found that the teenagers who reported that they had been taught to drink by their parents were drinking more often than those who had not been introduced to alcohol in this way. Other studies (e.g. Hingson and Kenkel 2004; York et al. 2004; Pitkanen et al. 2004) also suggest that young people who begin drinking early tend to drink more and report more binge drinking and drunkenness at 15–16 than those who start later:

> the kids know that if you're going to be criticizing them you're a hypocrite. Because it's, you know haven't, it's not a secret from my children that I've you know drunk to excess, and I've used drugs and most other things. So there's no question of getting pious about those kind of things, sometime I suppose I'd like my kids to be able to recognize certain, certain kind of, or to develop certain bodily habits and practices that would mean that they were sensible, yes, about whether they decided to get drunk.
>
> (Myles Huff, Stoke-on-Trent, 45–54, Male, NS-SEC 1)

> [Discussing his daughter starting University in the next year] I'm not worried, no. I mean she's grown [up], she's [been] going to the pub with us from being not very old and she's had an odd drink. I think if she'd never had a drink before [she] went straight to college you'd go berserk, if you'd never had a drink. Where[as] she's grown up and she knows what effect it has on her and she does occasionally have a few drinks but I mean she's like me, she doesn't like having a bad head or she's ill. She's quite sensible … because she's been to pub with us since she's been young, she's had a glass of wine [since] she's been 15, 16 with a meal and so occasionally had a few and had a bad head in the morning.
>
> (Gary Bellis, Eden, 45–54, Male, NS-SEC 3)

The youth generation present themselves as having a responsible attitude to alcohol including a belief that they 'know their own limits' (cf. Honess et al. 2000). It is a view supported by most of their parents (mid generation) who described trusting their children to manage their own drinking and to make their own mistakes. As such, when the youth generation have returned home drunk their parents have been being accepting of this 'rite of passage' rather than being angry or punitive in the way that the mid generation recalled their own parents' responses to similar practices:

> I can just remember coming through the front door and Mum smiling at me and saying 'Have you been drinking?' I said 'Yes' and she said 'Well as long as you know what you're doing' kind of thing, so it was. I think there was that, she passed on the responsibility to me because she knew I wasn't an idiot.
>
> (Adam Huff, Stoke-on-Trent, 18–24, Male, NS-SEC 2)

> Peter: I mean when we were like 16 or 17 if we wanted to go out on a Thursday the rule was you go out, you don't drink too much and you get up for school the next morning. That was the rule and if I didn't go to school then I wasn't allowed to go out ... And Mum, definitely when we were younger, Mum or our other friends' Mum would come and pick us up at the end of the night ... They've not been strict ...

> Interviewer: Is that a sensible approach? I mean obviously it's a few years away but if you had kids do you think you'd go down the same road?

> Peter: Probably at the end of the day they're [kids] going to get hold of drink somehow aren't they? So if you ease them in, I don't know how to term it but if you kind of ... regulate how they drink and steadily increase their sensibility on how much they can drink then it probably works best ... because ... if you restrict somebody, if my parents had said to me I couldn't drink and stuff and I'd have gone to Uni I probably would have gone a bit mental.
>
> (Peter Kirkland, Eden, 18–24, Male, NS-SEC 5)

> Interviewer: And did your Mum or Dad ever guess that you'd been doing that or ever catch you going in drunk?

> Gail: ... Well I don't know, I think my parents were quite liberal really, sort of just let her get on and do her own particular thing and [make] her own mistakes and things ... We were just sort of like, I don't know, they just didn't seem to be bothered, they used to laugh at us really.
>
> (Gail Cox, Stoke-on-Trent, 18–24, Female, NS-SEC 2)

Amongst the Pakistani Muslim informants some of the older and mid generation interviewees regarded the consumption of alcohol by some young men within their community as a negative product of integration (i.e. 'drinking is part of the British way of life'). These interviewees suggested that such patterns represent a break with the community's collective traditions, and evidence of more individualized lifestyles that are characteristic of contemporary British society. However, traditional 'norms' and values in any culture evolve over time. As such, it does not necessarily follow that the signs of change described above necessarily mean a weakening of intergenerational relations and an inevitable move towards individualization within Pakistani Muslim communities in the UK. Indeed, the youth generation interviewees did not regard drinking by young men within the Pakistani Muslim community as evidence of such generational change. Rather, those that were, or had previously experimented with alcohol, argued that drinking is temporary phase that was not necessarily incompatible with having a personal faith. Instead, these interviewees suggested that drinking often occurs when young people are in their late teens to early twenties and 'naturally' experiment with their identities and lifestyles at a time when their lives are less circumscribed by traditional commitments and responsibilities but that on marriage, family duty (particularly the importance of not tarnishing the family's honour) and social/community obligations must outweigh individuals' personal interests and desires (Yip 2004) and that at this point young people stop drinking. As we show in Chapter 5, interviewees suggest that such alcohol consumption by some members of the Pakistani Muslim youth generation represents a normal process of transition to adulthood, rather than a significant generational shift in attitudes and behaviour within the community. While the interviews with the older and mid generations demonstrated that there is awareness across the Pakistani Muslim community of a degree of 'hidden' drinking within the community, this is not acknowledged publicly, or within families (except sometimes between siblings). As such, parenting practices have not changed in line with the more relational approach adopted in wider British society. Rather, informants from all three generations described a parenting culture still predicated on a traditional hierarchical model of parental authority and deference by young people with relatively little open intergenerational dialogue around the issue of alcohol:

> In the Pakistani culture it's a taboo to drink alcohol, it's seen as a sin. It's seen as a bad influence in your body, and the purity of you and your religion and what you believe. It can bring about conflict as well…people will talk about each other if it's bad [if you drink] and it gives you a bad name, gives the family a bad name, a reputation. So it is policed in that sense … some of the people [in the local Pakistani Muslim community] do know that some of the kids do drink but they don't make an issue of it as well if that makes sense. They let them go do because they think they're going to you know once they're married they'll be settled, and it's just a little phase they're going through … for women it's not the done thing is it, women are put on their pedestal aren't they and respect them. They've got to be pure …
>
> (Salima Mahomed, Stoke-on-Trent, 18–24, Female, NS-SEC 5)

Conclusion

The contemporary debate about 'binge drinking' in the UK has implicitly contained a representation of a growing social problem but while alcohol consumption is increasing, the evidence of this research is that this picture conceals a more complex pattern of continuity and change across three cohort generations. While the price of alcohol has fallen and the supply of alcohol increased (particularly off-trade sales, as well as the development of the night-time economy) nonetheless there are some striking continuities in drinking cultures across the three generations. Most notably, the evidence of our intergenerational interviews is that the age of young people's first drink amongst the majority population has remained strikingly similar for young men. Likewise, across all three generations young people have drunk underage behind their parents' backs both in marginal public spaces and/or either furtively/socially sanctioned in commercial venues. In this sense, alcohol has persistently been important to young people in the majority population.

However, the type of product that majority young people are drinking has changed significantly between the mid and youth generation (from beer and cider to a greater emphasis on spirits and shots). As a result young people are adopting similar patterns of behaviour to their parents during their own youth but are actually consuming significantly more units of alcohol through these practices. At the same time, the motivation to drink has also shifted significantly. Alcohol is no longer something occasionally shared with friends as an accompaniment for, but not essential to, a night-out but rather is itself now the impetus or rationale for getting together or going out: an agent of peer networks. As such, the youth generation are under far more peer pressure to drink heavily and in particular to get drunk than the older or mid generation recall they experienced. This pressure to 'have a good time' was experienced by the Pakistani Muslim interviewees as well as the majority interviewees. However, while women's alcohol consumption (at home and in public space) has significantly increased across the majority generations, as has the visibility of women drinking in public venues, nonetheless the relaxation of traditional gendered notions of 'respectability' has not kept pace with this discontinuity in gendered practices. Women from the majority population who drink to excess in public (at all ages) still face more opprobrium than men who do so. Likewise, within the Pakistani Muslim community drinking by young women is still taboo in contrast to that by young men which is tolerated as an 'absent presence' within the community.

As alcohol has become more commonplace within majority homes how parents attempt to establish rules about young people's drinking and communicate with them about alcohol has also changed. Within the majority population there has been a general extra-familial shift in the emphasis of parenting between cohort generations – from disciplining young people to enabling their expressivity – which has produced a notable change in the ways that attitudes and practices about alcohol are communicated in intra-familial contexts between family generations. Majority parents are now reluctant to exercise authority in the traditional way, but prefer to have an open dialogue with their children in an effort to introduce 'sensible' drinking habits at an early age. Whereas in the Pakistani Muslim community parenting styles remain largely unchanged, despite some evidence of increased levels of drinking in secret by a minority of young men within this community as part of 'normal' transitions to adulthood.

These patterns of continuity and change have a number of potential policy implications. First, they indicate that the main drivers of patterns of change have been the alcohol and retail industries who have targeted emerging markets (young people and women) through the development of new products and night-time economy venues, as well as the development of off-trade sales – namely, the pricing and promotion of alcohol for home-based consumption (see also Kneale and French, 2008 on the need to diversify our focus on the sites where alcohol is consumed). Second, they suggest that public policy initiatives that seek to reduce young people's 'binge drinking' need to focus more explicitly on changing the motivation to drink – notably, to reduce the importance of alcohol within young people's social networks and particularly peer pressure to consume alcohol to excess. Finally, they indicate the need to evaluate the effectiveness of contemporary parenting strategies to instil sensible drinking habits in young people.

Here, the relationship between the mid and youth generations' drinking practices is significant. Mid generation interviewees commonly described how their own habits of drinking to excess in their youth had been tempered in mid-life as they had settled down, taken on the responsibilities of paid employment, mortgages and become parents. There is an implicit expectation that their children will also follow the same 'natural' transition. Likewise, the youth generation interviewees themselves were also quite dismissive about the health warnings associated with 'binge drinking'. This is consistent with other recent studies (Turning Point 2004; Engineer 2003; Richardson 2003; Balfe 2007) with young people which have also concluded that this generation perceive little risk associated with episodes of heavy drinking other than to their personal safety. The main reason for this is that while young people recognize the potential health dangers associated with heavy 'binge' drinking they do recognize themselves as potentially vulnerable to these consequences because they regard their own pattern of drinking as only a temporary phase in their life ('part of growing up', 'everybody does it'). They rationalize this by arguing that they have only been drinking for a short period of time (the last few years) and believe that at some point (most suggested their mid to late twenties) they will cut back their alcohol consumption. As such they consider that their current phase of heavy drinking will only constitute a small proportion of their life and that as such their drinking career will be too brief – when considered against their overall potential life span – to inflict any significant damage on their bodies and so they disregard public health warnings. Yet, this rationale does not allow for the fact that key elements of their patterns of drinking are significantly different to previous generations at this life-stage. They are: consuming significantly more units of alcohol because of the types of product they are drinking; drinking more alcohol at home as well as in public spaces; and face more peer pressure than the mid generation at the same age to get drunk, and as such may experience different long term health consequences than previous generations. Moreover, the evidence of the mid and older generation interviewees from the majority population in this study is that while patterns of consumption do change at different life-stages (i.e. people tend to drink different products, consume more alcohol at home than in public venues, and have different motivations to drink as they get older i.e. to relax or overcome domestic or workplace stress rather than to fit in with peers or have confidence with the opposite sex), nonetheless individuals consistently under-estimate how much they consume. In this sense, young people and parents' expectations that discontinuities in intergenerational patterns of drinking will provide 'natural' protection for the youth generation from the potential harms of drinking to excess are likely to be misplaced.

Chapter 7
Emotions and Bodies

In the preceding chapters of this book there have been a significant number of references to emotional and embodied issues bound up with alcohol, drinking and drunkenness. For example, Chapter 1 described the stigmatizing of working-class and young peoples drunken bodies in our cities; Chapter 2 described how feelings of isolation in rural areas can impact on adults drinking practices, Chapter 3 showed that people drink at home in order to unwind and relax in a 'safe atmosphere' and so on. However, despite emotions and bodies being addressed by a significant amount of writing about alcohol, drinking and drunkenness the topic has tended to be approached in an implicit manner. For example, research in the medical and health sciences has considered topics that include; the ways in which biological differences of men and women impact on alcohol consumption and drunkenness (Graham et al. 1998), how physiology affects drinking related anxieties (De Boer et al. 1993), and considered social-medial discourses relating to women who drink and 'flash' (Hugh Jones et al. 2000). Other studies have addressed alcohol, alienation and stress (Seeman et al. 1988). Nonetheless, beyond this work there has not been a sustained attempt to fully investigate the relationships between bodies and emotions and political, economic, social, cultural and spatial practices and processes relating to alcohol consumption. In this chapter we signpost a number of ways in which this agenda can be taken forward (see Jayne et al. 2010).

Emotional and Embodied Geographies of Alcohol Consumption

Studies of our emotional life are now a well established field of study in human geography. Work has focused on issues such as joy, sadness, confusion, excitement, fear, conviviality, love, hate, arousal, reciprocity and so on in order to understand the interplay between emotions, space and place (Davidson and Bondi 2004; McCormack 2003; Thrift 2004). In this writing emotions are considered as important elements of everyday life, and theorists have sought to look at 'embodied and mindful phenomena that partially shape, and are shaped by our interaction with people, places and politics that make up our unique, personal geographies' (Davidson and Bondi 2004, 373). For example, studies of emotional geographies have considered a fascinating range of case studies which includes, ageing and bereavement, women's responses to hysterectomies, the gendered psychodynamics of consumer culture (via a focus on food), and also how we can be 'moved' by nature (see Davidson et al. 2005).

Research has shown how emotions matter and sought to understand how they affect the ways we sense the substance of out past, present and future. Davidson and Bondi (2004) argue that emotions are integral to our sense of self, with socio-cultural circumstances dictating the ways in which different forms of emotional management are appropriate for particular social groups. Moreover, as Davidson et al. (2005) suggest our lives can be bright, dull or darkened by our emotional outlook. Writing has thus sought to understand how our emotional lives are articulated and bound up in complex negotiations based on 'socio-spatial mediation and articulation rather than as entirely interiorized subjective mental states' (Davidson et al. 2005, 10).

In terms of emotional geographies theorists have also sought to make intimate connections between the 'psycho-social and material boundaries through which embodied persons are differentiated from one another and from their surrounding environments' (Longhurst 2001, 7). Drawing on a large social science literature, research by geographers has considered a wide range of issues that include, 'ugly' and abject bodies, men's bodies in bathrooms, pregnant bodies, the body and chronic illness, old age, children and obesity and so on (see Kenworthy-Teather 1999; Longhurst 2001; Evans 2006, 2010; Evans and Colls 2009). Such writing shows how emotions reside in bodies and places and that there are relational flows, fluxes and currents, in-between people and places. Indeed, Longhurst (2001) argues that bodily boundaries are frequently perceived and negotiated in emotionally powerful as well as disruptive and conflictual ways. Feelings such as excitement, pride and pleasure, and/or guilt, shame and anger can thus be considered as key components of understanding geographies of alcohol consumption and drunkenness via consideration emotions and embodiment.

When read together writing on emotions and embodiment offers insights into the ways in which different types of alcohol affect different people in different places and spaces, and how such geographies are bound up with social mixing, personal interaction and the circulation of atmospheres, moods and feelings. For example, Phil Hubbard (2005) considers the experience of 'going out' in the 'evening economy' and shows how danger, unpleasantness, frustration, resentment, pleasure, desire, anger, happiness and fear can be key elements of a night out. Hubbard argues that the occasion of 'a big night out' is saturated with emotion and indeed that these emotions help us to make sense of particular spaces and places and how we manage our emotional selves. Although, not specifically investigating the impact of alcohol or degrees of drunkenness, Hubbard describes pleasure, embarrassment, emotional talk (arguing, comforting, romance and so on) as well as bodily discomforts bound up with drinking alcohol. Key to Hubbard's argument is the understanding that alcohol consumption generates intimate social relations, resistance, community, corporeal participation, sharing and is an key factor facilitating the 'togetherness' of a night out for both close-knit groups and by generating a broader shared experience with other revellers (see also Matthee 2004).

Comparing people's perceptions and experiences of going out in city centres in relation to out of town venues, Hubbard (2005) shows how different kinds of emotional management are required for 'big' or 'quiet nights' out. For some, city centres relate to feelings of excitement and/or anxiety, thought to be lively and stimulating and in these terms opposite to the polite and predictably relaxed and comfortable experience of visiting the cinema at an out of town retail park. As such, while emotions are both a state of mind and a physical experience, it is clear that 'particular encounters between self and world elicit a strong affective reaction which is emergent rather than pre-given (such as the embarrassment we experience when we arrive inappropriately dressed at an interview or presentation or the frustration we feel when technology doesn't work)' (Hubbard 2005, 120). Moreover, managing these emotions is part of the process by which we construct our sense of self, Hubbard asserts that theorists must take account of the socio-cultural circumstances dictating that particular forms of emotional management are appropriate for different social groups (for example, men and women manage their emotional selves differently, with men often expressing vulnerability). In summary, Hubbard suggests:

> it seems self evident that any understanding of emotional attachment to place must take into account the capabilities of the body ... corporality, bodily stature ... likewise inscriptions on the body, gendered classed, ages, sexed ... need to consider social meaning of the body alongside bio-medial understanding of corporeality, ... embodied ontology stresses that individuals are only able to express themselves in space through their bodies ... corporeal, physicality representing this as being in the world. (2005, 122)

Drinking and rowdiness associated with Hubbard's (2005) 'intoxicated geographies' of a 'big night out' can be described as a 'world of sensations, of movement, of the loss and recovery of physical control', or a 'collective body-for-fun' (Alan Radley 1995, 9). This shows that alcohol, drinking and drunkenness are 'not merely the private, subjective enjoyment of the body, but also a symbolic transformation of feeling with the body ... That is to say, they [drinkers] inhibit an imaginary world of their own making, central to which is their comportment and that of their fellows' (Radley 1995, 11). The street, loud and busy ensures transactions between people, places and things and understanding this milieu is clearly a fruitful topic for researchers. Hence, unpacking the relationship between peoples' drinking related practices and experience of space and place (underpinned by identity positions based on class, gender, ethnicity, sexuality and so on) and legislation, regulation and social relations and cultural practices is of great importance.

A further contribution to our understanding of embodied and emotional geographies can be seen in Latham and McCormack's (2004) discussion of the materialities surrounding alcohol, drinking and drunkenness. For example, Latham and McCormack address the physiological impact of alcohol (and other drugs) on issues such as conflict and violence, and the relationship between drunkenness and the ways that alcohol amplifies or focuses our experiences of particular spaces. They also highlight the importance of understanding the materialities of drink itself – sweetness, taste and texture – and identify the need for future research to address how specific drinks affect people in different ways. Latham and McCormack's (2004) ideas can thus be seen as a vital springboard from which to launch study of a whole range of potentially fruitful research topics relating to the materialities of embodied and emotional geographies of alcohol, drinking and drunkenness. Relevant work could include for example, study of the relationship between drinking and drunkenness and venues, furniture, lighting, music, drinking at home, in parks and gardens, the weather, the time of day and year and so on. There is clearly much work to be done to explore the co-constitutive relations between emotions embodiment, space and place and alcohol, drinking and drunkenness. An indicative list of possible future research topics includes the relationships between excitement, anticipation, apprehension, affection and sociability bound up with drinking. Hangovers, regret, sadness and 'boozer's gloom' as well the excitement, anticipation, apprehension, affection and sociability bound up with drinking, performativity and national, regional and local and identities are pertinent areas for study. Fun, spontaneity, confidence, sociability, beer jackets, (loosing) control, 'pulling', bloatedness, throwing-up, 'boozers gloom', 'auto-pilot', cuts and bruises, brewers droop and urinating in wardrobe sare just a selection of the topics raised in research presented throughout this book as being key to peoples drinking practices and experiences.

In this chapter we offer some examples that highlight how investigating the diverse and heterogeneous feelings, sensations and experiences of 'intoxicated geographies' can help us to better understand alcohol, drinking and drunkenness both within and beyond the discipline. In doing so we do not attempt to engage with the all possible avenues of research, but instead we focus on just three consideration of 'memories' (Anderson 2004a and b; Thrift 2004; Young 2002), 'rites of passage' (Kenworthy-Teather 1999) and 'emotional talk' (Mehta and Bondi 1999). In doing so we wish to address the artificial separation, and hence under-theorization of the relationships between emotions, embodiment and everyday uses of alcohol.

Memories

Recent work by Ben Anderson (2004) discusses how consumption of music is bound up with an artefactual mediation of memory, where things 'fit' with particular socio-spatial activities. Anderson describes practices of remembering which include the ephemeral and subject-less practice of 'involuntary remembering' in which a trace of a virtual past affects 'in itself', as well as 'intentional remembering, where a past is conditioned to occur as a fixed, relatively durable memory via the circulation and organization of affect. Such examples were clearly present in our respondents' use of alcohol. In these terms alcohol can work as a technique, to, or function for, the spacing and timing of memory. In other words there is a contextual, embodied practice of remembering which generates the symbolic content of 'a memory' (Thrift 2004)

For example, in our research in Stoke-on-Trent and Eden, respondents from all social groups reflected on the substance of memories of parties, holidays and so on, by focusing on certain family members, places and times and specific alcoholic drinks. In particular, memories of moments of heightened emotions, jollity, fun, silliness, relaxation, closeness and togetherness are presented as being facilitated and at least partially remembered because of the role of alcohol. As Young (2002, 87) argues parents offer children models of how to be embodied in the form of corporeal dispositions suggesting that, 'within families memory is passed down, not only as oral lore or material artefacts but also as ... corporeal dispositions'. As the following comments show there is a clear sense of remembrance, fondness and appreciation of the role that drinking and drunkenness can play in framing family and other social relations:

> this would be in nineteen fifty, fifty one, about that, I remember that being, father had come back from the War and he used to go to the Rugby Club on Saturday afternoon ... we used to go out and watch, he used to have a few drinks at the club, and I can recollect the players in the changing rooms afterwards, getting ready, changing after the game, having showers and the pints of beer after the game ... [edit] And I remember my father buying them ... [edit] The beer ... 'cos he's very keen on sports. Secondly I can remember my father having a bottle of beer, Usher's beer in home in Chippenham, I mean in his chair and, yes, that's one of my recollections, and it's early, you know. He used to go out, we used to, this would have been round about when I was seven or eight, he used to go out with a relative to the, to the pub, you know, Farringdon, Berkshire and he used to go out for a drink in the evening, Christmastime, it was Boxing Day or Christmas Eve, round about Christmas time, and be a long time in the pub and I was taken, I was given the privilege of going with him, but I had to say outside the door, wait outside the door while they drunk ... [edit] And stand there. Waiting for them, you know for a couple of hours.
>
> (Maurice Haige, Stoke-on-Trent, 55–64, Male, NS-SEC 4)

> Actually, I think it was really, really young because the alcohol in China is very popular and especially in the festival, like Chinese New Year or maybe like people have the newborn baby, they obviously make a special rice wine for everyone, so I think when I was a few years old I did try, my mother and me, we went to her friends house and her friend had a newborn baby and they make extra special rice wine and I had and I was drunk.
>
> (Shaung Lai, Stoke-on-Trent, 25–34, Female, NS-SEC 7)

In contrast, some respondents' recollections of the impact of alcohol on family life and relationships reflected less happy memories and feelings. Arguments, tensions, danger and domestic abuse and violence as well as individuals own drinking experiences in their families can clearly be seen to have a long term resonance:

> it was boxing day and I was fourteen and we was at my Grandma and Grandad's and I got paralytic and had to go home with my dad and I spoilt the day for everyone ... [edit] Just because I ... I spilt a vase of flowers and I was sick in toilet and that sort of thing and it's seen as inappropriate.
>
> (Rowena Birdwell, Stoke-on-Trent, 18–24, Female, NS-SEC 7)

> The one that really sticks out [edit] ... Christmas, my brother was offered a sip of brandy by my mum and he swigged the whole lot and this caused major hassle in our house, and since then he's been completely teetotal, he's not touched a drop of alcohol since.
>
> (Allan Cummins, Stoke-on-Trent, 25–34, Male, NS-SEC 4)

> I've never drunk because of my dad. He worked in the steelworks [edit] at closing time every night I used to open the front door and watch my father stagger or crawl across the road, fall in through the front door and then collapse on the floor. It has quarry tiles so he used to wake up freezing cold in the middle of the night and stumble up to bed ...
>
> (Stoke-on-Trent Local Authority Councillor)

Anderson's description of embodied skill, revolving around habitual remembering, intuition and mimicry is clearly present in these accounts of memories of alcohol and drunkenness. Respondents also talked about mundane acts of selecting a bottle or certain type or brand of drink, their responses to the sound of a 'pop' of a cork or the opening of a can of beer, to holding a glass and executing the 'correct' pouring of different drinks, of cutting and adding fruit and ice as evoking re-occurring and involuntary memories of previous drinking experiences, without internal recollection – part of the 'not yet' conscious background to everyday life (Anderson 2004). However, the selection of certain drinks, tastes, or visiting specific places or commercial venues are also depicted as being part of a process of intentionally remembering – so that the past comes to be implicated or experienced in the 'now' through the organization of affect (Anderson 2004). In these terms Anderson suggests that there are complex and interrelated emotional and embodied links 'to remembering' via the senses. Respondents also talked about engagement with objects that are prosthetic companions that act and afford from within practices of remembering and forgetting.

In these terms an intertwining of liquids, objects, people, places and non-rational modalities of emotion and affect, of moods and feelings allowed respondents to express the place of memory in past, present and future experiences of alcohol and drunkenness. The taste and smell of certain drinks triggered memories of good or bad times, groups and individual replaying and retelling of drinking practices, drinking games, of songs sung too loudly. As such a whole range of experiences are enacted through contemplative drinking and its associated emotional and affective intensity – how drinking 'feels right', or relates to the sensing of sexual experiences, of laughter of friends remembering. Of course, these techniques of remembering also include trying to piece together memories via sensations and guess work and that a key element of alcohol is being too drunk to remember.

Rites of Passage

Intimately bound up with such 'memory work' was respondents' reflections on certain 'rites of passage' that relate to alcohol consumption. This included geographies of personal discovery, and rich and intriguing experiences and encounters relating to certain 'ritual crossing of a threshold ... not necessarily a symbolic one ... a physical separation of the activity of one group from those of another' (Kenworthy-Teather 1999, 13). For example, respondents reflected on teenage 'out of control' drunkenness (Winchester et al. 1999), the movement through adolescence to 'legal' drinking, and moving away from home (see Valentine et al. 2009a; Holloway et al. 2009), their concern for older people's alcohol consumption because of physical/mental frailty, or social isolation (Hugman 1999; Teo 1999). However, central to these stories of 'rites of passage' involve alcohol consumption as allowing the use of, and learning about new types of spaces and places as well as being key to the evolution and performance of identity.

For example, respondents talked about negotiating access to alcohol, either given by parents or naughtily stolen. Central to this was the feeling of 'being treated like an adult' or 'tying out adult activities' in family contexts. Recollections then often moved to first experiences of explicitly 'adult behaviour' away from the family, of feeling (and being viewed as), old enough, or confident enough to purchase alcohol from off licences, pubs and nightclubs. In the quotes below, respondents described the excitement, naughtiness, and newness of such experiences as important moments of engaging with adulthood, quickly followed by the imperative of learning how to behave as drunk (being able to 'hold' your drink, or mask the effects of alcohol) and of being able to hide drunkenness from their families. One key component of such early drinking was the importance of drinking to cementing relationships in friendship groups. Risk and trust, were considered as vital to friendships bound up with the getting, consuming together (even sharing the same bottle or can) and hiding underage drinking.

> The first time I drank on my own. I actually stole a, a liqueur, it was in a really fancy bottle. From my grandma's cupboard. With my friends, and of course got absolutely hammered and was sick everywhere, I poured it, because I couldn't put it anyway, obviously you can't take it back half drank. So, yeah, so we drank all of that, and then, that carried on, we used to do that on a weekly basis. She used to have this cupboard just full. My granddad used to make wine, you know had loads of fruit juice, we used to take whatever we could and like, you

know we used to Johnny Mack, which is really expensive whisky, we used to take it to the park and neck it. Yeah, basically, we'd drink anything ... [edit] Oh yeah, yeah, and then word got about, you know we'd get it and everyone would come up there. I can remember like once we all went back to my nan's house, pretending we needed the toilet and we put all this drink down our trousers, all of us, like this and walk out like this. [laughs] Oh I think she knew but she was just so soft, she wouldn't say anything.

(Ann Peters, Stoke-on-Trent-on-Trent, 25–34, Female, NS-SEC 1)

The emotional ties that alcohol offers in terms of sociability and friendship were also noted as key to feelings of 'freedom' and independence, for example, in moving from the family home for work or to attend university, of being a key ingredient in sexual experience or in starting/ending relationships. Other respondents talked about the ways in which changing emotional priorities due to child care or work responsibilities led to reduced drinking. Nonetheless, when relationships with friends and family bound up with alcohol consumption changed, respondents also reflected on the loss of past pleasures:

I used to be a premier league drinker. Each week, I'd get paid, put my rent to one side and then put £160 a week aside for drink. I'd go out with my friends and they would say after 10–12 pints how come you're not drunk. I started drinking at my local pub when I was 15, they knew I was underage but turned a blind eye as long as I was not trouble. If I stepped out of line I would have got a battering from the older men for causing a disturbance. My family, it used to be a big day of the week, something I will always remember, on Sunday afternoons we would get all dressed up as if we were going to church and go to the pub for a few hours before dinner – I liked that. I stopped drinking when I got a serious relationship, others had failed 'cos of how much I drank, but I made the effort and I got a new job, and you can't drive a taxi when your pissed or hung over not with the traffic like it is.

(Male Bar Worker, Stoke-on-Trent)

Yes, I used to have a local near where I lived I went in it for 30 years, and there was 6 of us that always used to sit together on the same table – it was a table meant for 4 but we sat at it had a copper top and always wobbled. It was always six people, some came and went over the years but it was always six regulars who sat together – even if the rest of the pub was empty we used to sit at that table and put the world to rights – it was known as our table and no-one ever sat at it apart from us. I moved away and at first I used to drive down but then you can only have a couple and everyone else if having 5 or 6 you feel left out, so I've stopped going. I popped in last year and my place had been taken but there was still six men, now all in there sixties that sat there.

(Carl Allan, Stoke-on-Trent, 65+, Male, NS-SEC 7)

Such quotes resonate with Philo et al.'s (2002) research into alcohol and mental health noted in Chapter 2 which investigates the symbolic contribution of drinking around issues such as conviviality, hospitality, relaxation and drinking 'as a reward'. This research investigates both the important symbolic contribution of drinking to regional identity, but also how excessive drinking and drunkenness are an accepted and important element of local social relations. Elaborating on this position, Philo et al. show how alcohol is bound up with emotional geographies around a number of issues. These include hospitality, a lack of leisure opportunities, relaxation and a reward, coping strategies and both isolation and belonging. They also show the ways in which these geographies are gendered, with men's heavy drinking tending to take place in public whilst women's heavy drinking is more private and solitary and thus a constitutive element of exclusionary social relations.

Similar, elements of exclusionary social relations was represented in our findings (see also Holloway et al. 2009). For example, Doris, a working woman of pensionable age suggested that prior to her husband's death that they were regular visitors to their local pub. Although she enjoys the feelings of relaxation that alcohol offers, Doris suggested that the pleasure of going to the local pub was because of the 'the crack' and that it allowed people to 'keep in touch with everybody':

> I really miss the crack and keeping up with everybody really. It's not seemly for a woman of my age to walk down and go in the pub on her own. Well I don't do it. I mean I'm only 62 but perhaps I'm, I'm thinking that. And something they've done with a lifetime companion, and then all of a sudden they are on their own, you know you back off ...
>
> (Doris Humphreys, Eden, 65+, Female, NS-SEC 7)

What begins to emerge from these different 'rites of passage' associated with alcohol consumption is an emotional and embodied and sense of 'belonging'. For example, although some respondents suggested that you could feel 'out of place' in venues by feeling to too old or too young in relation to others, and that some feared gendered, racist or homophobic comments and violence, or felt uncomfortable in pubs that they didn't know well, most respondents talked about being able to feel 'at home' in different places because of alcohol consumption. Such responses were also aligned with closeness with people, for example, people they may have know for many years, to friendships that emerge for just a few minutes, and brief interactions with strangers on the streets (see Jayne et al. 2010). The diversity of such relations were expressed in the following quotes, where (not so) intimate social relations offer people a sense of community, corporeal participation, sharing – and are a key factor in facilitating the 'togetherness' of a night out for close-knit groups and for a broader sense of shared experience with other drunken revellers (see also Matthee 2004):

Once a month and those tend to generally be the best nights because what, quite
often I'll play but so will lots of other friends but it'll end up with virtually
everybody playing and some sort of free for all singing and the pub ... [edit]
it's the atmosphere and the fun that I want, it's, the alcohol helps to sort of relax
you but it is a, it is pure, it is a secondary part of it, it's talking, it's actually the
conversations with friends that, that I like.

(Malcolm Patterson, Stoke-on-Trent, 55–64, Male, NS-SEC 4)

And people you don't know from Adam, what they do for a living you know,
you can sit and talk to them for half an hour and the next thing you can go back
in and go oh how's your daughter, you know how's your wife, blah blah blah
and it's really nice to talk to people just like, it's like a big social venue, you just
go oh hello how are you?

(Ann Peters, Stoke-on-Trent, 25–34, Female, NS-SEC 1)

I go in the pub, I don't mind going in the pub on my own. Or to meet, to, on the
off chance that somebody I know will be in there. And I can, you know catch
up on, on some news. ... [edit] You don't feel as though, oh I haven't been,
I haven't been there for like you know sort of like, a week, I'd better go in
quick in case everybody's forgotten, forgotten who I am you know, that sort of,
that sort of thing. I think sometimes you feel, you almost feel as though you're
committed to the pub, you want the pub to succeed. [edit] But the other side is
the sort of camaraderie that's, that you, you sort of, you know miss. The, it's
like a sort of camaraderie and it's also a sort of a mutual thing, sort of help, help
thing, there's always help.

(Maurice Haige, Stoke-on-Trent, 55–64, Male, NS-SEC 4)

Respondents acknowledged that such *feelings of belonging and social
interaction were to a large degree facilitated by alcohol.* Moreover, what was clear
from the research is that drinking loosens inhibitions, offers the opportunity for
creative and innovative thinking, allows the opportunity to say things you might
not usually – all of which were considered as part of the pleasure of drinking.
Indeed, the feeling of abandonment and being able to 'loose' yourself (Wood
2002), was often expressed in terms of and enjoyment of the suspension of 'real
time' into 'pub time' – of whiling away the hours – or in terms of heightened sexual
desire and enjoyment of loud music and spectacular lighting (Malbon 1999). For
example, respondents talked (ether affectionately or in terms of embarrassment)
about having 'beer goggles' – of finding others interesting to talk to, or attractive
and sexy – and of being less judgemental of strangers, and that being able to
overcome social boundaries was often described as emotionally liberating.

Emotional Talk

Such examples can be conceptualized in terms of people's dulled/slowed/ heightened embodied emotions caused by bio-chemical and psychological responses to alcohol in conjunction with an interaction with social and shared affects of belonging and connectivity with friends and strangers (see Jayne et al. 2010). Respondents reflected that such experiences were, in part, performed through 'emotional talk' (Mehta and Bondi 1999). For example, the following quote illustrates the psychological responses to the combination of drinking and chatting with friends prior to a night out helps the respondent deal with the stresses of the week so that the night out can be free from worry:

> And I usually don't work on Fridays, it's only just recently I've started so, we'd start with a bottle of wine … about half one, two, open the wine, you know, why not, talk about the day, chill out, and then we'll start getting ready to go out. And then the vodka comes out … at my house, yeah, and then we'll get the vodka, sometimes if we're feeling particularly cheeky, we'll have a couple of little bottles of alcopops … and then we'll open the vodka and then get ready, drink as we're getting ready. And people come, people come to my house and meet us there, and we'll drink vodka all together and then we'll go out and then we'll drink when we get back as well. And so you'd be chatting about what the night's going to be like or where you're going or what kind of stuff? Yeah, yeah, and what we did last week, I mean it's not really changed from … we'll talk about work as well, as we unwind, we'll talk about work and what's happened there, because my friend has got quite a stressful job as well and we sort of really offload on each other and get it all out, then we're ready to go out. And, but generally we'll just, we will talk about work to start off with and just check everyone's had a good week and looking at the events that have happened and then we'll get on to the subject of what we're going to do, where we're going to go and then when we're out, we talk about the … I'm sure if you recorded it, it'd sound stupid … dead stupid. [laughs]
>
> (Ann Peters, Stoke-on-Trent, 25–34, Female, NS-SEC 1)

Emotional talk, thus enhances the affects of alcohol and its performance of cementing 'closeness' in a number of ways – from listening to friends' drunken silliness, rants and melancholy as well as drunken conversations with strangers. In addition to this the spatial/physical proximity of people consuming alcohol is important to the affect of extended time sitting around a table in pubs, in public spaces and domestic spaces was regarded as important, whether as part of a group, or one-to-one discussions. Thus, alcohol consumption combined with the time spent in particular space which facilitated interaction is considered as key times for uninterrupted and often candid communication.

However, this was not always convivial. All respondents also acknowledged that emotional talk may involve confrontations, losing one's temper, being argumentative, belligerent, stubborn and so on. For some, this happened when alcohol amplified an existing mood or offers an opportunity to express long running feelings about certain people or topics:

> Ann: But if mentally, you're really up for it and you want to be you know bit a devil, lairy and have a good night then, yeah, that. I really think that it's all down to what sort of mood you're in ... [edit] Yeah, if you drink gin. Then tears, but that's great though, because, it's great, because it's hilarious the next day, it's. Liz, Liz has been my best friend since I was sixteen years old. And we're really close friends and we know each other really well, [laughs] We'll sit there and just cry and cry and cry and she's just like, and you know at the time, you think oh there's something wrong with me, I can't stop crying, and it's like, it's connected to your hormones and everything but it's quite healthy sometimes .. [edit] To let it all out and it's fine ... [edit] Sometimes I can be really mouthy in a horrible way to people. I just get really ... and I'm just being vile to people. Very cutting ... [edit]

> Interviewer: And do you ever have to apologise the next day or do you feel guilty about it?

> Ann: Well, yes and that happened to me a couple of weeks ago, actually, I got really drunk and I was really out of order with a friend of mine, and I woke up the next morning, I really cringed. [edit] And I rang him straight away, I said I'm really sorry and he said oh no it's fine, don't worry about it.
>
> (Ann Peters, Stoke-on-Trent, 25–34, Female, NS-SEC 1)

> Your capacity to make an arse of yourself, you can drink and drink when you're out the house and just in the past I've done that and I don't know, just I'd got to the point where I just didn't like waking up the next day thinking what have I done and what have I said? Even though it was none, just that sort of, that feeling you get the next day after ale.
>
> (Allan Cummins, Stoke-on-Trent, 25–34, Male, NS-SEC 4)

Despite such conflicts and tensions related to the freedom of expression associated with drinking, and what some people referred to as 'beer fear' – the uncomfortable feeling of trying to remember what might have happened or been said the night before – such experiences were tempered by an emotional reciprocity, where bad behaviour, melancholy and so on is more often than not forgiven amongst friends. The ability to discount such behaviour as being 'down to the drink', was also acknowledged as bringing people together and strengthening relationships, of getting to know the best and worst of people through their drunkenness, of expressions both good and bad of peoples behaviour in terms of remembering, forgiving or forgetting.

Conclusion

In this chapter we have considered just three ways in which a focus on emotional and embodied geographies associated with alcohol, drinking and drunkenness add value to an understanding of the combination of biochemical and physiological impulses as well as the social and cultural mediation of performative experiences (see Jayne et al. 2010). In conceiving of alcohol consumption in terms of (non) human and spatial relations; modes of embodiment and expression of practices; in considering the ways in which drinking transform the ways bodies connect with other bodies and objects and spaces (in terms of actual physical and/or perceptual experiences of contexts); and how alcohol consumption is an active quest to experience certain 'feelings' in specific contexts we have sought to offer examples of interventions into a challenging yet fruitful area of research. The complex and often unpredictable nature of alcohol consumption was presented by respondents in our research as a central feature of their challenging, unpredictable, fun, sad, and often un-rememberable 'intoxicated geographies' and we suggest that this area of research is deserving of sustained theoretical, empirical and policy attention.

Afterword
'One for the Road?'

This book contributes to research into geographies of alcohol, drinking and drunkenness which addresses the interpenetration of; the production, regulation (e.g. brewing, distributing, marketing and selling as well as legislation, planning, policy and policing) and consumption of *alcohol* (purchasing and drinking); the social, cultural and material practices and experiences bound up with *drinking* alcohol and, the physiological, psychological and biological nature of how intoxication is experienced, performed and represented through *drunkenness* (Jayne et al. 2008). In doing so we have sought to formulate and signpost a research agenda which builds on the work of handful of theorists from across the discipline, including cultural, social, historical, medical, political and economic geographers who have in specific ways and with differing degrees of focus and depth considered alcohol, drinking and drunkenness. Although it is disappointing that geography have been relatively slow to engage with alcohol, drinking and drunkenness recent work by geographers has nonetheless included theoretical and empirical contributions which have much to offer alcohol research.

In investigating *(dis)orderly spaces* we have argued that while alcohol research has included geographical perspectives, studies have nonetheless tended to under theorize the ways in which space and space are key constituents of alcohol, drinking and drunkenness. For example, work undertaken by scholars in a variety of disciplines including the medical and health sciences, psychology, sociology, politics, criminology and cultural studies have considered issues relating to alcohol via 'geographical' issues such as spatial scale, national, regional and local identities, distinctions between public and private, urbanity and rurality, boundaries and transgressions, visibility and invisibility, centrality and marginality and so on. In these terms a large amount of rich, detailed and relevant geographical work has been undertaken by alcohol researchers relating to a diverse set of topics, social groups and spaces and places. However, this case study approach has meant that alcohol research have overwhelmingly failed to pursue connections, similarities, differences and mobilities between case studies and as such consideration of space and place has been undertaken via a de facto and/or fragmented agenda that has tended to depict drinking in an abstract way that while being based on particular people or places does not enable generalizations to be made. In these terms research which has had a geographical focus has rarely moved beyond specificities and has thus failed to generate a convincing case to assert the importance of geography as a key feature of alcohol research.

In contrast, and despite being a relatively fledgling disciplinary agenda geographers' consideration of alcohol, drinking and drunkenness has produced *both* rich and detailed case study research *and* theoretically nuanced studies. At its very best the study of alcohol, drinking and drunkenness undertaken by geographers has attempted to challenge an ontological and epistemological impasse where alcohol is conceived on the one hand as a medical issues involving the pathologization of alcohol as a health, social, legislative, crime or policy problem, and on the other hand as a practice embedded in social and cultural relations. Each chapter in this volume has thus sought to highlight the ways in spatial thinking and geographical imaginations offer insights which add value to understanding of the political, economic, social, cultural and spatial practices and processes bound up with alcohol, drinking and drunkenness.

The first three chapters, for example, focus on the city, the countryside and home. These chapters highlight how 'problematic', 'sensible', 'safe' and 'unsafe' drinking practices, and the spaces and places where alcohol consumption takes place are differentially and discursively constructed in relation to each other. In these terms, the ideological dimensions that constitute notions of, for example, the countryside and home and associated geographies of alcohol consumption were shown to relate to visions of violence and disorder associated with urban drinking. In a similar vein, the subsequent chapters focused on gendered, ethnic and generational drinking patterns and practices highlighting not only similarities and differences across social groups, but also how alcohol consumption in particular spaces and places is considered and/or experienced as problematic (or not) for those social groups. In the final substantive chapter of the book, we also show how a focus on emotional and embodied knowledges and experiences relate to, and help to understand alcohol consumption by different social groups in specific spaces and places. We argue that embodied and emotional geographies offer insights into alcohol, drinking and drunkenness insights not previously addressed in alcohol research. The chapters in *Alcohol, Drinking and Drunkenness* thus engage with issues such as legislation, policy and policing; production, marketing and retail; consumption, identity, lifestyle and forms of sociability in ways that allows connections between different people, places, practices and processes, addressing similarities, differences, connectivities and mobilities at a variety of different transnational, national, regional and local spatial scales to be pursued. Throughout the pages of this volume we have aimed to highlight and celebrate work that challenges the ontological and epistemological understanding of alcohol, drinking and drunkenness *and* which explicitly contributes to theoretical debates both within and beyond the discipline of geography.

Despite the progress made by geographers there is nonetheless much work to be done to assert the importance of studying alcohol, drinking and drunkenness within the discipline. Moreover, as well as championing the importance of geography to alcohol research agendas – through the usual routes of research monographs, articles in interdisciplinary journals, conference presentations and so on – it is also vital that geographers offer theoretical and empirical interventions into political and popular debates. To this end, while we toast geography for joining the party, in this book we have sought to challenge human geographers from all areas of study, and alcohol studies researchers engaging in 'geographical' issues and approaches, to build on the progress already made in order to achieve a critical, sustained and coherent approach to studying geographies of alcohol, drinking and drunkenness.

Appendix 1
Case Studies and Research Design

The research on which this book is based was conducted in two contrasting geographical communities. Stoke-on-Trent is a deprived urban area with higher than national average levels of alcohol consumption and a changing consumption landscape. The District of Eden, Cumbria, is an isolated rural area where the centrality of the pub in village life has historically been linked with the development of a strong temperance movement.

Stoke-on-Trent

Stoke-on-Trent, a city of around 250,000 people is located in the English Midlands and sits between Birmingham and Manchester. This is a traditional working class area, that today experiences significant levels of deprivation. This deprivation takes multiple forms. Economically, the area has higher than national average levels of unemployment, and a significant proportion of the population have no qualifications (43 per cent of. national average of 29 per cent). Deprivation is also reflected in the health of the local population: mortality is higher than average in this area, as is the prevalence of limiting long term illness (24 per cent cf. national average 18 per cent) (ONS, 2001). Stoke-on-Trent has a significant population from minority ethnic groups. For example, the proportion of the population who identified themselves as Pakistani in the 2001 census is nearly double the national average (ONS, 2001). There is also a significant population of asylum seekers. North Staffordshire has been specifically identified as a cluster area in the National Asylum Support Service's dispersal policy.

Stoke-on-Trent's *Community Strategy* promotes the night-time economy as part of its regeneration agenda. Between 1997 and 1999 the capacity of Stoke-on-Trent's licensed premises rose by 242 per cent; this period also saw a 225 per cent rise in assaults associated with night-time drinking. Recent figures show that out of 354 local authority areas in the UK Stoke-on-Trent is ranked in the highest quartile for alcohol specific hospital admissions and for alcohol related months of life lost (North West Public Health Observatory, Local Alcohol Profiles for England 2006). Within Stoke-on-Trent's City Centre there are 18 public houses which are licensed to sell alcohol up to 23.00hrs and 28 special hour certificate premises which are licensed to sell alcohol into the early hours, usually until 02.00hrs. There are 13 off licenses, 26 licensed restaurants and 16 fast food late night refreshment house premises. The combined capacity for the bars and nightclubs within the City Centre is approximately 25,000 people. In spring 2003 the City Council introduced an on-street alcohol ban for the city centre in response to alcohol related disorder. Indeed, a MORI postal survey on adult lifestyles has shown that drinking levels in North Staffordshire are akin to that of the North West which has the highest average rates of consumption in the country. Alcohol Concern has also identified a specific local problem of binge drinking among young people.

Eden, Cumbria

Eden, is the most sparsely populated district in England and Wales. It has a population of over 50,500 people: 15,500 of these live in Penrith, the largest urban centre; some others are clustered in 3 other small towns which each have populations of 2–3,000 people; but over 50 per cent of the local population is scattered in small villages. Like many rural areas in Britain the population here is overwhelmingly white (99.6 per cent), over 80 per cent identify themselves as Christian, and no other religion accounts for more than 0.2 per cent of the population.

The area, which has a stable although relatively low-wage economy, falls into the middle-ranks of tables measuring deprivation: however, these average figures hide a great deal. Whilst the nature of the housing market in urban areas means geographical pockets of deprivation emerge, the same is not true of isolated rural areas where households on differing levels of income are quite likely to live in the same village. These average figures hide then both the existence of rural poverty (and wealth) and also obscure the different ways in which deprivation is experienced in the country as opposed to the city.

The area is particularly interesting in terms of alcohol use. Traditionally the pub has been one of the few social spaces open to rural residents, and it continues to be important in many villages today (although home-based consumption patterns may be significant). The prevalence of drinking in this area in the past, along with the strength of Methodism, led to the development of an active temperance movement which both taught about the dangers of drink and provided a practical alternative to the pub as a social space (e.g. organizing the building of village halls). Temperance parades and temperance clubs for children continued to be a feature in the area into the 1990s, organized under the auspices of the Vale of Eden Band of Hope Union.

Today levels of alcohol use here are lower than the national average. Recent figures show that out of 354 local authority areas in the UK Eden is ranked in the lowest quartile for alcohol related months of life lost (men), alcohol related violent offences and alcohol related recorded crime (North West Public Health Observatory, Local Alcohol Profiles for England 2006). As in other areas these average figures hide significant variation by social group. A recent health authority survey found that Cumbrian women consumed 6.4 units of alcohol per week while Cumbrian men drank on averages 17.2 units of alcohol (both figures exclude non-drinkers). Moreover, it found that alcohol consumption is higher amongst 16–35 year olds than amongst older residents.

There were five elements to the research:

Historical and Contemporary Geographies of the Case Study Areas

We undertook specific archival work on the history of drinking cultures in Stoke-on-Trent and Eden. This included: mapping the geography of licensed drinking establishments through council records (where available); exploring the reporting of drink as a social issue/problem in the local print media; and an examination of the local temperance movement through archival sources.

The contemporary pattern of drinking in the two case study areas was captured through a telephone survey administered by a social research company. Five hundred people completed the questionnaire survey in each geographical location. The social research company purchased telephone numbers from Datalynx using the following criteria (within the specified geographic regions): name, address and telephone number, aged 18+. The data was captured in the following ways: the numbers were acquired from the electoral roll in the first instance and then filtered against the deceased register, bereavement register, gone away register before being tele-appended using BT Osis to verify that names match with addresses, and to append the phone numbers. The survey was devised with reference to national surveys and significantly modified to suit the aims of the project. The survey was piloted through a random sample of 15 people, and was re-drafted in response to this pilot and in the light of comments from members of the project's advisory group.

The Interviews were recorded and transcribed using conventional social science techniques. All the names of people and venues in the report have been changed to protect the anonymity of the research participants.

Participant Observation in Consumption Spaces

The different spaces in which alcohol is consumed in each of the case study areas were mapped by a researcher carrying out participant observation. This process involved the researchers recording both descriptive observations (about the space; the numbers and types of clientele; general activities and specific acts; ambience etc.) and a narrative account to build up an overall picture of each of the establishments that they visited. Participant observation was also carried out by the researchers on key streets in each case study area at different times of the night/week to develop a picture of the night-time economy and the relationship between alcohol, public cultures and the civility of the streets.

Interviews with Key Informants

In-depth taped interviews were conducted with key stakeholders in each of the two localities to explore the positive and negative features of alcohol consumption.

Interviews and Photo-diaries with Residents

On the basis of the telephone survey 20 residents were recruited for interview from each of the case-study areas to reflect the socio-economic diversity of the local population and a range of attitudes to, and use of alcohol (as described in the survey). In addition, a further 10 participants from the Pakistani community in Stoke-on-Trent were interviewed in order to explore the issues as they relate to this particular ethnic minority group. Given the potential cultural and language issues, we employed, and trained, a researcher from the community to undertake these interviews.

To begin participants were given the opportunity to use a disposable camera to keep a photo-diary of their alcohol use and/or leisure activities which do not involve the consumption of alcohol. Where returned these photographs were subsequently used in interviews to promote discussion about the participants' attitudes to, and use of alcohol.

The interviews explored: (1) *Establishing behaviour*: first memories of alcohol; family and peer context in early alcohol use; access issues; (2) *Patterns and cultures of drinking*: type/level of alcohol consumption; when and where alcohol bought and consumed; family and peer contexts; what drunk; where/when/with whom; relationship of alcohol consumption to the use of other substances (3) *Attitudes to alcohol*: do they like it; what stops them drinking more/less; who approves/disapproves of their consumption; attitudes to drunkenness/binge drinking; physical feelings around consumption; health; role in their social life; (4) *Wider attitudes to alcohol*: benefits of drinking; problems associated with alcohol use; tensions within family/peer groups about alcohol use. (These themes were adapted for abstainers/low users).

Case Studies of Intergenerational Change in Drinking Habits/Cultures

Interviews were also conducted with 2 and where possible 3 generations of the same family. We focused on 5 case-study families in each area: each of the family members was interviewed individually to maintain confidentiality within the families and thus help ensure openness. In order to explore potential gender variations in these intergenerational changes we followed the male line in some case-study families and the female line in others. The families were chosen from a diversity of class, and in Stoke-on-Trent also ethnic, backgrounds. These interviews explored the different generations' experiences of: learning about alcohol, establishment of drinking practices, consumption spaces, wider social attitudes to alcohol, health promotion messages, and intergenerational conflict.

The multi-methods approach implemented during this research project has ensured that a large amount of data has been collected. As such, not all of the archival material, in-depth interviews and participant observation can be presented in this book. However, while the data presented here does represent only a fraction of the material gathered it has been specifically chosen too reflect the larger body of evidence.

Appendix 2
Definition of Binge Drinking and Guide to Alcohol Unit Measurements

In 1995 the UK Government report *Sensible Drinking* changed the guidelines for recommended limits from a weekly to a daily measure of consumption, reflecting the concern that: 'weekly consumption can have little relation to single drinking episodes and may indeed mask short term episodes which ... often correlate strongly with both medial and social harm'. The change from an emphasis on weekly to daily levels does not increase the recommended upper limit for weekly consumption.

The current Department of Health advice is that men should not drink more than 3–4 units of alcohol per day, and women should not drink more than 2–3 units of alcohol per day. 'Binge drinking' is less clearly defined, but has been referred to be the Department of Health and Office for National Statistics as 'consuming eight or more units for men and six or more units for women on at least one day during the week'. In other words double the daily recommended levels of consumption.

One unit of alcohol is measured as 10ml of pure alcohol and guidance is given in terms of particular drinks As a rough guide, the following unit measurements apply:

- One pint of ordinary strength lager: 2 units
- One pint of strong lager: 3 units
- One pint of bitter: 2 units
- One pint of ordinary strength cider: 2 units
- One small (175ml) glass of wine: 2 units approx
- One measure of spirit: 1 unit
- One alcopop: 1.5 units approx

It is however very difficult to be accurate as measures, strengths and types of alcohol vary considerably.

Appendix 3
UK Governments' National Statistics Socio-Economic Classification

1. Managerial and professional occupations;
2. Intermediate occupations;
3. Small employers and own account workers;
4. Lower supervisory and technical occupations;
5. Semi-routine and routine occupations;
6. Never worked and long term unemployed;
7. Unclassified.

Bibliography

Abad, L.C. (2001), 'Gender and Drink in Aragon, Spain', in de Garine, I. and De Garine, V. (eds), *Drinking: Anthropological Approaches* (New York: Bergham Nook), pp. 144–157.

Ahmed, A. (2003), *Islam under Siege* (Cambridge: Polity Press).

Ahmed, N. (1989), 'Service Provision for Ethnic Minority Drinkers from an Asian Background', Published in proceedings of 35th *International Congress on Alcoholism and Drug Dependence Prevention and Control: Realities and Aspirations*, Waahlberg, R. (ed.) (National Directorate for the Prevention of Alcohol and Drug Problems, Oslo), pp. 37–44.

Aitchison, C., Hopkins, P. and Kwan, M-P. (2007), *Geographies of Muslim Identities: Diaspora, Gender and Belonging* (Aldershot: Ashgate).

Alam, M.Y. and Husband, C. (2006), *British-Pakistani Men from Bradford: Linking Narratives to Policy* (York: Joseph Rowntree Foundation Report).

Alavaikko, M. and Osterberg, E. (2000), 'The Influence of Economic Interests on Alcohol Control Policy: A Case Study from Finland', *Addiction* 93, Supplement, 4: S565–S579.

Allaman, A., Voller, F., Kubicka, L. and Bloomfield, K. (2000), 'Drinking and the Position of Women in Nine European Countries', *Substance Abuse* 21/4: 231–247.

Ambert, A. (1994), 'An International Perspective on Parenting: Social Change and Social Constructs', *Journal of Marriage and the Family* 56: 529–43.

Anderson, B. (2004a), 'Recorded Music and Practices of Remembering', *Social and Cultural Geography* 5/1: 3–20.

Anderson, B. (2004b), 'Time-stilled Space Slowed: How Boredom Matters', *Geoforum* 35: 739–754.

Anderson, B. (2006), 'Becoming and Being Hopeful: Towards a Theory of Affect', *Environment and Planning D: Society and Space* 24: 733–752.

Arber, S. and Attias-Donfut, C. (2000), *The Myth of Generational Conflict: the Family and State in Ageing Societies* (London: Routledge).

Atkinson, R. (2003), 'Domestication by Cappuccino or a Revenge on Urban Space? Control and Empowerment in the Management of Public Spaces', *Urban Studies* 40/9: 1829–1843.

Atlay, C. (2008), 'Possibilities of Reconfiguration: Sustaining Creative Use in Urban Space', *Urban Design* 108: 34–36,

Attias-Donfut, C. (1988), *Sociologie des Générations, L'empreinte du Temps* (Paris: PUF).

Bakhtin, M. (1984), *Rabelais and His World*, translated by H. Iswolsky (Bloomington: Indiana University Press).

Balfe, M. (2007), 'Alcohol, Diabetes and the Student Body', *Health, Risk and Society* 9: 241–257.

BBC News (2007), 'Wealthy Areas Head Alcohol Table', 16.10.2007 (http://news. bbc.co.uk/1/hi/health/7045830.stm) accessed 22 November

Beccaria, F. and Sande, A. (2003), 'Drinking Games and Rites of Life Projects: A Social Comparison of the Meaning and Functions of Young Peoples Use of Alcohol During the Rite of Passage to Adulthood in Italy and Norway', *Youth* 11/2: 99–119.

Beck, U. and Beck-Gernsheim, E. (2002), *Individualization* (London: Sage).

Becker, H. (1966), *Outsiders: Studies in the Sociology of Deviance* (New York: Free Press).

Beckingham, D. (2008), 'Geographies of Drink Culture in Liverpool: Lessons from the Drink Capital of Nineteenth-century England', *Drugs: Education, Prevention and Policy* 15/3: 305–313.

Belina, B. and Helms, G. (2003), 'Zero Tolerance for the Industrial Past and Other Threats: Policing and Urban Entrepreneurialism in Britain and Germany', *Urban Studies* 40/9: 1845–1867.

Bell, D. (2005), 'Commensality, Urbanity, Hospitality', in Lashley, C., Lynch, P. and Morrison, A. (eds), *Critical Hospitality Studies* (London: Butterworth Heinemann), pp. 24–35.

Bell, D. (2007), 'The Hospitable City: Social Relations in Commercial Spaces', *Progress in Human Geography* 31: 7–22.

Bell, D. and Binnie, J. (2005), 'What's Eating Manchester? Gastro-culture and Urban Regeneration', *Architectural Design*: 29–36.

Benson, D. and Archer, J. (2002), 'An Ethnographic Study of Sources of Conflict between Young Men in the Context of a Night Out', *Psychology, Evolution and Gender* 4/1: 3–30.

Berman, M. (1986), 'Take it to the Streets: Conflict and Community in Public Space'. *Dissent* (Summer): 476–485.

Berns McGown, R. (1999), *Muslims in the Diaspora* (Toronto: Toronto University Press).

Bianguis-Gasser, I. (1992), 'Wine and Men in Alsace, France', in de Garine, I. and De Garine, V. (eds). *Drinking: Anthropological Approaches* (New York: Bergham Nook), pp. 101–107.

Bloomfield, K. (1993), 'A Comparison of Alcohol Consumption between Lesbians and Heterosexual Women in an Urban Population', *Drug and Alcohol Dependence* 33: 257–269.

Blunt, A. and Dowling, R. (2006), *Home* (London, Routledge).

Bobak, M., Mckee, M., Rose, R. and Marmot, M. (1999), 'Alcohol Consumption in a Sample of the Russian Population', *Addiction* 94/ 4: 857–866.

Body-Gendrot, S. (2000), *The Social Control of Cities: A Comparative Perspective* (Oxford: Blackwell).

Bogenschneider, K., Wu, M-Y., Raffaeli, M. and Tsay, J.C. (1998), '"Other Teens Drink, but Not My Kid": Does Parental Awareness of Adolescent Alcohol Use Protect Adolescents from Risky Consequences', *Journal Marriage and the Family* 60/2: 356–373.

Boseley, S. (2007), 'Scale of Harmful Middle-class Drinking Revealed', *The Guardian* 16 October, p. 12.

Bradby, H. (2007), 'Watch Out For the Aunties! Young British Asians' Accounts of Identity and Substance Abuse', *Sociology of Health and Illness* 29: 656–672.

Brannen, J., Moss, P. and Morley, A. (2004), *Working and Caring over the 20th Century* (Basingstoke: Palgrave Macmillan).

Brennan, P.L. and Greenbaum, M.A. (2005), 'Functioning, Problem Behaviour and Health Services Use among Nursing Home Residents with Alcohol-use Disorders: Nationwide Data from the VA Minimum Data Set', *Journal of Studies on Alcohol* 66: 395–400.

Brickell, K. (2008), '"Fire in the House": Gendered Experiences of Drunkenness and Violence in Siem Reap, Cambodia', *Geoforum* 39/5: 1667–1675.

Bromley, R.D.F. and Nelson, A.L. (2002), 'Alcohol-related Crime and Disorder across Urban Space and Time: Evidence from a British city', *Geoforum* 33/2: 239–54.

Bromley, R.D.F., Tallon, A.R. and Thomas, C.J. (2003), 'Disaggregating the Space-time Layers of City Centre Activities and their Users', *Environment and Planning A.* 35: 1831–1851.

Bromley, R.D.F., Thomas, C.J. and Millie, A. (2000), 'Exploring Safety Concerns in the Night-time City', *Town Planning Review* 71: 71–96.

Bunce, M. (1994), *The Countryside Ideal: Anglo-American Images of Landscape* (London: Routledge).

Burnett, J. (1999), *Liquid Pleasures: A Social History of Drinks in Modern Britain* (London: Routledge).

Burns, N., Parr, H. and Philo, C. (2002), 'Alcohol and Mental Health: Social Geographies of Rural Mental Health', Findings Paper 12 (http://web.ges.gla. ac.uk/Projects/WebSite/FP12Alcohol.pdf).

Campbell, H. (2000), 'The Glass Phallus: Pub(lic) Masculinity and Drinking in Rural New Zealand', *Rural Sociology* 65/4: 562–581.

Castree, N. (2005), 'The Epistemology of Particulars: Human Geography, Case Studies and Context', *Geoforum* 36: 541–544.

Chatterjee, P. (2003), 'An Empire of Drink: Gender, Labour and the Historical Economies of Alcohol', *Journal of Historical Sociology* 16/ 2: 183–208.

Chatterton, P. and Hollands, R. (2002), 'Theorising Urban Playscapes: Producing, Regulating and Consuming Youthful Nightlife City Spaces', *Urban Studies* 39/1: 95–116.

Chatterton, P. and Hollands, R. (2003), *Urban Nightscapes: Youth Culture, Pleasure Spaces and Corporate Power* (London: Routledge).

Clarke, P. (1983), *The English Alehouse: A Social History 1200–1830* (London: Bloomsbury).

Cochrane, R. and Bal, S. (1990), 'The Drinking Habits of Sikh, Hindu, Muslim and White Men in the West Midlands: A Community Survey', *British Journal of Addiction* 85: 759–769.

Cohen, P. (1997), *Rethinking the Youth Question* (London: Macmillan).

Coleman, J.S. (1988), 'Social Capital in the Creation of Human Capital', *American Journal of Sociology* 94: 95–120.

Comedia (1991), *Out of Hours: A Study of the Economic, Social and Cultural Life in Twelve Town Centres in the UK* (in association with Calouste Gulbenkian Foundation).

Conway, K.P., Swenden, J.D and Merikangas, K.R. (2002), 'Alcohol Expectancies, Alcohol Consumption, and problem Drinking: The Moderate Role of Family History', *Addictive Behaviours* 28: 832–836.

Cresswell, T. (1996), *In Place/Out of Place: Geography, Ideology and Transgression* (Minneapolis, MN: University of Minnesota Press).

Cunningham, H. (1980), *Leisure in the Industrial Revolution 1780–1880* (New York: St Martin's Press).

Davidson, J. and Bondi, L. (2004), 'Spatializing Affect; Affecting Space: An Introduction', *Gender, Place and Culture* 11/3: 373–374.

Davidson, J., Smith, M. and Bondi, L. (eds) (2005), *Emotional Geographies* (Aldershot: Ashgate).

Davis, J. and Ridge, T. (1997), *Same Scenery, Different Lifestyle: Rural Children on Low Income* (London: The Children's Society).

Davis, M. (1991), *City of Quartz* (London: Verso).

Day, K., Gough, B. and McFadden, M. (2004), '"Warning! Alcohol Can Seriously Damage your Feminine Health": A Discourse Analysis of Recent British Newspaper Coverage of Women and Drinking', *Feminist Media Studies* 4/2: 165–183.

De Boer, M., Schippers, G.D., Van der Staak, C.P.F. (1993), 'Alcohol and Social Anxiety in Women and Men: Pharmacological and Expectancy Effects', *Addictive Behaviour* 18: 117–126.

De Garine, I. (2001), 'Drinking in Northern Cameroon amongst the Masa and Muzey', in de Garine, I. and De Garine, V. (eds), *Drinking: Anthropological Approaches* (New York: Bergham Nook), pp. 51–65.

De Garine, I. and De Garine, VC. (eds) (2001), *Drinking: Anthropological Approaches* (New York: Bergham Nook).

Dean, A (2002), 'History, Culture and Substance Use in a Rural Scottish Community', *Substance Use and Misuse* 37/5–7: 749–765.

DeVerteuil, G. and Wilton, R.D. (2009), 'The Geographies of Intoxicants: From Production and Consumption to Regulation, Treatment and Prevention', *Geography Compass* 3/1: 478–494

Douglas, M. (ed.) (1987), *Constructive Drinking* (Cambridge: Cambridge University Press).

Dwyer C. (1999), 'Veiled meanings: young British Muslim women and the negotiation of difference', *Gender, Place and Culture* 6: 5–26.

Dwyer C. (2000), 'Negotiating Diasporic Identities: Young British South Asian Muslim Women', *Women's Studies International Forum* 23: 475–486.

Eber, C. (2000), *Women and Alcohol in a Highland Maya Town: Water of Hope, Water of Sorrow*, updated edition (Austin: University of Texas Press).

Edensor, T. (2006), 'Caudan: Domesticating the Global Waterfront', in Bell, D. and Jayne, M. (eds) *Small Cities: Urban Experience Beyond the Metropolis* (London: Routledge), pp. 46–59.

Edwards, W. (1997), *Potters in Pubs* (Leek: Churnet Valley Books).

Eldridge, A. and Roberts, M. (2008), 'Hen Parties: Bonding or Brawling?', *Drugs: Education, Prevention and Policy* 15/3: 323–328.

Engineer, R., Phillips, A., Thompson, J. and Nicholls, J. (2003), *Drunk and Disorderly: a Qualitative Study of Binge Drinking Among 18–24 year olds* (London: Home Office).

Ettore, E. (1997), *Women and Alcohol: A Private Pleasure or Public Problem?* (London: The Women's Press).

European Comparative Alcohol Study 1998–2001 (2002), Brussels: European Union.

European Schools Project on Alcohol and Drugs 1995–2003 (2003), Brussels: European Union.

Evans, B. (2006), '"Gluttony or Sloth": Critical Geographies of Bodies and Morality in (Anti)obesity Policy', *Area* 38: 259–267.

Evans, B. (2010), 'Anticipating fatness: Childhood, Affect, and the Pre-emptive 'War on Obesity', *Transactions of the Institute of British Geographers* 35/1: 21–38.

Evans, B. and Colls, R. (2009), 'Measuring Fatness, Governing Bodies: The Spatialities of the Body Mass Index (BMI) in Anti-Obesity Politics', *Antipode* 41/5: 1051–1083.

The Evening Sentinel (1986), 'The state of crown bank', reproduced in *The Way We Special*, p. 15.

The Evening Sentinel (1978), 'Great Annual Spree and Ale was Dirt Cheap', 6 August.

Featherstone, M. (1991), *Consumer Culture and Postmodernity* (London: Sage).

Foucault, M. (1977), *Discipline and Punish: The Birth of the Prison* (London: Allen Lane).

Foxcroft, D.R. and Lowe G. (1996), 'Adolescent Drinking Behaviour and Family Socialization Factors: a Meta-analysis', *Journal of Adolescence* 14: 255–273.

Frisby, D. (2001), *Cityscapes of Modernity* (Cambridge: Polity Press).

Fyfe, N. and Banister, J. (1996), 'City Watching: CCTV Surveillance in Public Spaces', *Area* 28: 37–46.

Galen, L.W. and Rogers, W.M. (2004), 'Religiosity, Alcohol Expectancies, Drinking Motives and their Interaction in the Prediction of Drinking Among College Students', *Journal of Studies on Alcohol* 65: 469–476.

Galvani, S. (2006), 'Alcohol and Domestic Violence: Women's Views', *Violence Against Women* 12: 641–662.

Gefou-Madianou, D. (1992), *Alcohol, Gender and Culture* (London: Routledge).

Ghost, S. (1984), 'Prevalence Survey of Drinking Alcohol and Alcohol Dependence in the Asian Population in the UK', in Krasner, N., Madden, J.S. and Walker, R.J. (eds) *Alcohol Related Problems* (Chichester: Wiley), pp. 179–189.

Giddens A. (1991), *Modernity and Self-Identity. Self and Society in the Late Modern Age* (Cambridge: Polity Press).

Gill, J.S. and Donaghy, M. (2004), 'Variation in the Alcohol Content of a "Drink" of Wine and a Spirit poured by a Sample of the Scottish Population', *Health Education Research* 19/5: 485–491.

Girouard, M. (1975), *Victorian Pubs* (London: Yale University Press).

Glendinning, A., Nuttall, M., Hendry, L.B, Kloep, M. and Wood, S. (2003), 'Rural Communities and Well-being: A Good Place to Grow Up?', *Sociological Review* 51/1: 129–156.

Gmel, G., Bloomfield, K., Ahlstrom, S., Choquet, M. and Lecomte, T. (2000), 'Women's Roles and Women's Drinking: A Comparative Study in Four European Countries', *Substance Abuse* 21/ 4: 249–264.

Goddard, E. (2008), *General Household Survey 2006: Smoking and Drinking Among Adults, 2006* (Newport: Office for National Statistics).

Gofton, L. (1990), 'On the Town: Drink and the 'new' Lawlessness', *Youth and Policy* 29: 33–39.

Graff, V. (2007), 'I didn't go to a dinner party until I was in my thirties', *The Observer*, 27 May, p. 12.

Graham, K., Wilsnack, R., Dawson, D. and Vogeltanz, N. (1998), 'Should Alcohol Consumption Measures be Adjusted for Gender Differences', *Addiction* 93/8: 1137–1147.

Gullestad, M. and Segalen, M. (eds) (1997), *Family and Kinship in Europe* (London: Pinter).

Habermas, J. (1974), *The Structural Transformation of the Public Sphere: Inquiry into a Category of Bourgeois Society* (Cambridge: Polity).

Hadfield, P. (2006), *Bar Wars: Contesting the Night in Contemporary British Cities* (Oxford: Oxford University Press).

Hagan, J. (1977), *Disreputable Pleasures* (New York: McGraw Hill).

Hall, T. (1992), *The Postmodern Pub, Hegemonic Narrative, Nostalgia and Collective Identity in the Construction of Postmodern Landscapes: A Problem for Research*, Discussion paper, Department of Geography, University of Birmingham.

Hall, T. and Hubbard, P. (1996), 'The Entrepreneurial City: New Urban Politics, New Urban Geographies', *Progress in Human Geography* 20: 153–174.

Hannigan, J. (1998), *Fantasy City: Pleasure and Profit in the Postmodern Metropolis* (London: Routledge).

Hansen, E.C. (1976), 'Drinking to Prosperity: The Role of Bar Culture and Coalition Formation in the Modernization of the Alto Panádes', in J.C. Aceves (ed.),

Economic Transformation and Steady State Values: Essays in the Ethnography of Spain (Flushing, NY: Queens College Press), pp. 42–51.

Harnett, R., Thom, B., Herring, R. and Kelly, M. (2000), 'Alcohol in Transition: Towards a Model of Young Men's Drinking Styles', *Journal of Youth Studies* 3/1: 61–77.

Harring, S. (1983), *Policing a Class Society: the Experience of American Cities 1865–1915* (New Jersey: Rutgers University Press).

Harrison, B. (1971), *Drink and the Victorians* (London: Faber).

Harrison, L. and Carr-Hill, R. (1992), *Alcohol and Disadvantage amongst the Irish in England* (Dublin: Federation of Irish Societies).

Harrison, L., Harrison, M. and Adebowale, V. (1996), 'Drinking Problems among Black Communities', in Harrison, L. (ed.), *Alcohol Problems in the Community* (London: Routledge), pp. 223–240.

Hasan, A.G. (2001), *American Muslims: The New Generation* (New York: Continuum).

Heim, D., Hunter, S.C., Ross, A.J., Bakshi, N., Davis, J.B., Flatley, K.J. and Meer, N. (2004), 'Alcohol Consumption, Perceptions of Community Responses and Attitudes to Service Provisions: Results from a Survey of Indian, Chinese and Pakistani People in Greater Glasgow, Scotland, UK', *Alcohol and Alcoholism* 39/3: 220–226.

Heley, J. (2008), 'Rounds, Range Rovers and Rurality: The Drinking Geographies of a New Squirarchy', *Drugs: Education, Prevention and Policy* 15/3: 315–321.

Herring, R. and Thom, B. (1997), 'The Right to Take Risks: Alcohol and Older People', *Social Policy and Administration* 31: 233–246.

Hingson, R. and Kenkel, D. (2004), 'Social Health and Economic Consequences of Underage Drinking in National Research Council and Institute of Medicine', in idem (eds), *Educating Underage Drinking: a Collective Responsibility of Background Papers* (Washington, DC: The National Academies), pp. 351–382.

HM Government (2004), *Alcohol Harm Reduction Strategy for England* (http://www.homeoffice.gov.uk/documents/Alcohol-strategy).

HM Government (2007), *Safe. Sensible. Social: the Next Steps in the National Alcohol Strategy* (http://www.homeoffice.gov.uk/documents/Alcohol-strategy).

Hobbs, D. (2003), *The Night-time Economy* (London: Alcohol Concern Research Forum Papers).

Hobbs, D., Hadfield, P., Lister, S. and Winslow, S. (2003), *Bouncers: Violence and Governance in the Night-time Economy* (Oxford; Oxford University Press).

Hobbs, D., Hall, S., Winlow, S. and Lister, S. (2000), 'Receiving Shadows: Governance, Liminality in the Night-time Economy', *British Journal of Sociology* 51: 701–717.

Hoffman, M. Richmond, J., Morrow, J. and Salomone, K. (2002), 'Investigating 'Sense of Belonging' in First Year College Students', *Journal of College Student Retention: Research, Theory and Practice* 4: 227–256.

Holder, H.D. (2000), 'The Supply Side Initiative as an International Collaboration to Study Alcohol Supply, Drinking and Consequences: Current Knowledge, Policy Issues and Research opportunities', *Addiction* 95/4, S416–S463.

Holliday, R. and Jayne, M. (2000), 'The Potters Holiday', in Edensor, T. (ed.) *Reclaiming Stoke-on-Trent: Leisure, Space and Identity in The Potteries* (Stoke-on-Trent: Staffordshire University Press), pp. 117–200.

Holloway, S.L., Jayne, M. and Valentine, G. (2008). '"Sainsbury's is my Local": English Alcohol Policy, Domestic Drinking Practices and the Meaning of Home', *Transactions of the Institute of British Geographers* 33: 532–547.

Holloway, S.L., Valentine, G. and Jayne, M. (2009), 'Masculinities, Femininities and the Geographies of Public and Private Drinking Landscapes', *Geoforum* 40/5: 821–831.

Holt, M.P. (ed.) (2006), *Alcohol: A Social and Cultural History* (London: Berg).

Honess, T., Seymour, L. and Webster R. (2000), *The Social Contexts of Underage Drinking* (London: Home Office).

Hopkins, P. (2006), 'Youthful Muslim Masculinities: Gender and Generational Relations', *Transactions of the Institute of British Geographers* 31: 337–352.

Hopkins P. (2007), 'Young People, Masculinities, Religion and Race: New Social Geographies', *Progress in Human Geography* 31: 163–177.

Hubbard, P. (2002), 'Screen-shifting: Consumption, 'Riskless Risks' and the Changing Geographies of Cinema', *Environment and Planning* A. 34: 1239–1258.

Hubbard, P. (2005), 'The Geographies of 'Going Out': Emotions and Embodiment in the Evening Economy', in Davidson, J. Bondi, L. and Smith, M (eds) *Emotional Geographies* (Aldershot, Ashgate), pp. 117–134.

Hughes, K., Anderson, Z., Morleo, M. and Bellis, M.A. (2008), 'Alcohol, Nightlife and Violence: The relative Contributions of Drinking before and During Nights Out to Negative Health and Criminal Justice Outcomes', *Addiction* 103: 60–65

Hugh-Jones, S., Gough B. and Littlewood, A. (2000), 'Sexual Exhibitionism Can be Good for You: A Critique of Psycho-medical Discourses from the Perspective of Women who Exhibit', *Sexualities* 8/3: 259–281.

Hugman, R. (1999), 'Embodying Old Age', in Kenworthy-Teather, E. (ed.), *Embodied Geographies: Spaces, Bodies and Rites of Passage* (London: Routledge), pp. 193–207.

Hunt, G.P (1991), 'The Middle Class Revisited: Eating and Drinking in an English Village', *Western Folklore* 50/ 4: 401–420.

Hunt, G.P. and Satterlee, S. (1981), 'Darts, Drink and the Pub: The Culture of Female Drinking', *Sociological Review* 3: 272–601.

Hunt, G.P. and Satterlee, S. (1986), 'Cohesion and Division: Drinking in an English Village', *Mankind* 21/3: 521–537.

Hunt, G. and Satterlee, S. (1986), 'The Pub, the Village and the People', *Human Organisation* 54/1: 62–74.

Hunt, G.P. Mackenzie, K. and Joe-Laider, K. (2005), 'Alcohol and Masculinity: The case of Ethnic Youth Gangs', in Wilson, T. M (ed.), *Drinking Cultures* (Oxford: Berg), pp. 225–254.

Hutchinson, I.W. (1999), 'Alcohol, Fear, and Woman Abuse', *Sex Roles* 40: 893–920.

Iveson, K. (2006), 'Strangers in the Cosmopolis', in Binnie, J., Holloway, J., Millington, S. and Young C. (eds), *Cosmopolitan Urbanism* (London: Routledge), pp. 36–47.

James, A. (1993), *Childhood Identities: Self and Social Relationships in the Experience of the Child* (Manchester: Manchester University Press).

Jamieson, L. and Toynbee, C. (1989), 'Shifting Patterns of Parental Authority, 1900–1980', in Corr, H. and Jamieson, L. (eds), *The Politics of Everyday Life* (London: Macmillan), pp. 56–67.

Järvinen, M. and Room, R. (eds) (2007), *Youth Drinking Cultures: European Experiences* (Aldershot: Ashgate).

Jayne, M., Holloway, S.L. and Valentine, G. (2006), 'Drunk and Disorderly: Alcohol, Urban Life and Public Space', *Progress in Human Geography* 30/4: 451–468.

Jayne, M. Valentine, G. and Holloway S.L. (2008a), 'Geographies of Alcohol, Drinking and Drunkenness: A Review of Progress, *Progress in Human Geography* 38: 247–264

Jayne, M., Valentine, G. and Holloway, S.L. (2008b), 'Fluid Boundaries – 'British' Binge Drinking and 'European' Civility: Alcohol and the Production and Consumption of Public Space', *Space and Polity* 12/1: 81–100.

Jayne, M., Valentine, G. and Holloway S.L. (2008c), 'The Place of Drink: Geographical Contributions to Alcohol Studies', *Drugs: Education, Prevention and Policy*, 1–14.

Jayne, M. Valentine, G. and Holloway S.L. (2010), 'Emotional, Embodied and Affective Geographies of Alcohol, Drinking and Drunkenness', *Transactions of the Institute of British Geographers* 35/4: 540–554.

Jones, J. (2002), 'The Cultural Symbolisation of Disordered and Deviant Behaviour: Young People's Experiences in a Welsh Rural Market Town', *Journal of Rural Studies* 18: 213–217.

Jones, M. and Jones, D. (2000), 'The Contagious Nature of Antisocial Behaviour', *Criminology* 38: 25–47.

Kelly, A.B. and Kowalyszyn, M. (2002), 'The Association of Alcohol and Family Problems in a Remote Indigenous Australian Community', *Addictive Behaviour* 28: 761–767.

Kenworthy-Teather, E. (1999), *Embodied Geographies: Spaces, Bodies and Rites of Passage* (London: Routledge).

Klein, N. (2000), *No Logo* (London: Flamingo).

Klostermann, K.C. and Fals-Stewart, W. (2006), 'Intimate Partner Violence and Alcohol Use: Exploring the Role of Drinking in Partner Violence and its Implications for Intervention', *Aggression and Violent Behaviour* 11: 587–597.

Kneale, J. (1999), '"A Problem of Supervision": Moral Geographies of the Nineteenth-century British Public House', *Journal of Historical Geography* 25/3: 333–348.

Kneale, J. (2001), 'The Place of Drink: Temperance and the Public 1856–1914', *Social and Cultural Geography* 2: 43–49.

Kneale, J. (2004), Drunken Geographies: Mass Observation's Studies of 'A Social Environment ... Plus Alcohol', 1937–48. Unpublished paper (available from author).

Kneale, J. and French, S. (2008), 'Mapping Alcohol: Health, Policy and the Geographies of Problem Drinking in Britain', *Drugs: Education, Prevention and Policy* 15: 233–249.

Knibbe, R.A. and Bloomfield, K. (2001), 'Alcohol Consumption Estimates in Surveys in Europe: Comparability and Sensitivity for Gender Differences', *Substance Abuse* 22/1: 23–38.

Komro, K.A. Maldonado-Molina, M.M., Tobler, A.L., Bonds, J.R. and Muller, K.E. (2007), 'Effects of Home Access and Availability of Alcohol on Young Adolescents Alcohol Use', *Addiction* 102: 1597–1608.

Kong, L. (2001), 'Mapping 'New' Geographies of Religion: Politics and Poetics in Modernity', *Progress in Human Geography* 25: 211–233.

Kraack, A. and Kenway, J. (2002), 'Place, Time and Stigmatised Youthful Identities: Bad Boys in Paradise', *Journal of Rural Studies* 18: 145–155.

Kubicka, L., Csemy, L., Duplinsky, J. and Kozeny, J. (1998), 'Czech Men's Drinking in Changing Political Climates 1983–93: A Three-wave Longitudinal Study', *Addiction* 93/8: 1219–1230.

Kumar, K. (1995), *From Post-industrial to Post-modern Society* (Blackwell: Oxford).

Kuusisto, A. (2007), 'Religious Identity Based Social Networks as Facilitators of Teenagers' Social Capital: A Case Study of Adventist Families in Finland', in Helve, H. and Bynner, J. (eds), *Youth and Social Capital* (London: Tufnell Press), pp. 787–106.

Lader, D. (2009), *Drinking: Adults' Behaviour and Knowledge in 2008* (Newport: Office of National Statistics).

Lader, D. and Goddard, E. (2006), *Drinking: Adults' Knowledge and Behaviour in 2006* (Newport: Office for National Statistics).

Lagendijk, A. (2003), 'Global "Lifeworlds" Versus Local "Systemworlds": How Flying Winemakers Produce Global Wines in Interconnected Locales', *Tijdschift Voor Economische en Sociale Geographie* 95/5: 511–526.

Lash, S. and Urry, J. (1994), *Economies of Sign and Space* (London: Sage).

Latham, A. (2003), 'Urbanity, Lifestyle and Making Sense of the New Urban Cultural Economy: Notes from Auckland, New Zealand', *Urban Studies* 40: 1699–1724.

Latham, A. and McCormack, D.P. (2004), 'Moving Cities: Rethinking the Materialities of Urban Geographies', *Progress in Human Geography* 28: 701–724.

Laurie, N., Dwyer, C., Holloway, S.L. and Smith, F.M. (1999), *Geographies of New Femininities* (Harlow: Addison Wesley Longman).

Laurier, E. and Philo, C. (2004), *Cafés and Crowds*. Published by the Department of Geography and Geomatics, University of Glasgow.

Laurier, E. and Philo, C. (2006), 'Cold Shoulders and Napkins Handed: Gestures of Responsibility', *Transactions of the Institute of British Geographers* 31/2: 193–207.

Laurier, E. and Philo, C. (2006), 'Possible Geographies: A Passing Encounter in a Café', *Area* 38: 353–363.

Leib, R., Merikangas, K.R., Holfer, M., Pfister, H., Isensee, B. And Wittchen, H-U. (2002), 'Parental Alcohol Use Disorders and Alcohol Use and Disorders in Offspring: A Community Study', *Psychological Medicine* 32: 63–78.

Leifman, H. (2001), 'Homogenisation in Alcohol Consumption in the European Union', *Nordisk Alkohol and Narkotikatidskrift* 18: 15–30.

Levi, R. and Valverde, M. (2001), 'Knowledge on Tap: Police Science and Common Knowledge in the Legal Regulation of Drunkenness', *Law and Social Inquiry* 21/3: 819–846.

Leyshon, M. (2005), 'No Place for a Girl: Rural Youth Pubs and the Performance of Masculinity, in Little, J. and Morris, C. (eds), *Critical Studies in Rural Gender Issues* (Aldershot: Ashgate), pp. 104–122.

Leyshon, M. (2008), '"We're Stuck in the Corner": Young Women, Embodiment and Drinking in the Countryside', *Drugs: Education, Prevention and Policy* 15/3: 267–289.

Lieb, R., Merikangas, K.R., Hofler, M., Pfister, H., Isensee, B and Wittchen, H.U. (2002), 'Parental Alcohol Use Disorders and Alcohol Use and Disorders in Offspring: A Community Study', *Psychological Medicine* 32: 63–78.

Lindsay, J. (2005), *Drinking in Melbourne Pubs and Clubs: A Study of Alcohol Consumption Contexts* (Melbourne: Monash University).

Lister, S., Hobbs, D., Hall, S. and Winslow, S. (2000), 'Violence in the Night-time Economy; Bouncers: The Reporting, Recording and Prosecution of Assaults', *Policing and Society* 10/4: 283–402.

Longhurst, R. (2001), *Bodies: Exploring Fluid Boundaries* (London: Routledge).

Lovatt, A. and O'Connor, J. (1995), 'Cities and the Night-time Economy', *Planning and Practice Research* 10/2: 127–134.

Lowe, G., Foxcroft, D.R. and Sibley, D. (1993), *Adolescent Drinking and Family Life* (London: Harwood Academic Publishers).

McAndrew, C. and Edgerton, R.B. (1969), *Drunken Comportment: A Social Explanation* (London: Nelson).

McCormack, D. (2003), 'An Event of Geographical Ethics in Spaces of Affect', *Transactions of the Institute of British Geographers* 28/4: 488–507.

McKeigue, P.M. and Karmi, G. (1993), 'Alcohol Consumption And Alcohol-related Problems in Afro-Caribbean's And South Asians in the United Kingdom', *Alcohol and Addiction* 28/1: 1–10.

Malbon, B. (1999), *Clubbing: Dancing, Ecstasy and Vitality* (London: Routledge).

Malcomson, R. (1973), *Popular Recreations in English Society 1700–1850* (Cambridge: Cambridge University Press).

Mannheim, K. (1952), *Essays on the Sociology of Knowledge* (London: Routledge Kegan Paul).

Marquis, G. (2004), 'Alcohol and The Family in Canada', *Journal of Family History* 29/3: 308–327.

Mars, G. (1987), 'Longshore Drinking, Economic Security and Union Politics in Newfoundland, in Mary Douglas (ed.), *Constructive Drinking: Perspectives on Drink from Anthropology* (Cambridge University Press), pp. 91–101.

Mass Observation (1987), *The Pub and the People* (London: The Cresset Library).

Massey, D. (1989), *Spatial Divisions of Labour: Social Structures and the Geography of Production*, 2nd edn (Routledge: New York).

Massey, D. (1995), 'Masculinity, Dualisms and High Technology', *Transactions of the Institute of British Geographers* 20: 487–99.

Matthee, D.D. (2004), 'Towards an Emotional Geography of Eating Practices: An Exploration of the Food Rituals of Women of Colour Working on Farms in the Western Cape', *Gender, Place and Culture* 11/3: 437–443.

Matthews, T. Yaylor, M., Sherwood, K., Tuker, F. Limb, M. (2000), 'Growing Up in the Countryside: Children and the Rural Idyll', *Journal of Rural Studies* 12: 101–112.

Maye, D., Iibery, B. and Kneafsy, M. (2005), 'Changing Places: Investigating the Cultural Terrain of Village Pubs in South Northamptonshire', *Social and Cultural Geography* 6/6: 831–847.

Measham, F. (2006), 'The New Policy Mix: Alcohol Harm Minimisation and Determined Drunkenness in Contemporary Society', *International Journal of Drug Policy* 17: 258–268.

Mehta, A. and Bondi, L. (1999), 'Embodied Discourse: On Gender and Fear of Violence', Gender, *Place and Culture* 6: 67 –85.

Mental Health Foundation (2006), *Cheers? Understanding the relationship between alcohol and mental health* (http://www.mentalhealth.org.uk/publications?EntryId=38566andq=0%c2%acalcohol%c2%ac640400%c2%ac2006%c2%ac)

Merrifield, A. (2000), 'The Dialectics of Dystopia: Disorder and Zero Tolerance in the City', *International Journal of Urban and Regional Research* 24/2: 473–489.

Michalak, L., Trocki, K. and Bond, J. (2007), 'Religion and Alcohol in the U.S. National Alcohol Survey: How Important is Religion for Abstention and Drinking?', *Drug and Alcohol Dependence* 87/2–3: 268–280.

Miles, S. (2000), *Youth Lifestyles in a Changing World* (Buckingham: Open University Press).

Miles, S. and Paddison, R. (1998), 'Urban Consumption: An Historical Note', *Urban Studies* 35/5–6: 815–832.

Miller, W.B. (1958), 'Lower-class Culture as a Generating Milieu of Gang Delinquency', *Journal of Social Issues* 14/3: 5–19.

Mintel (2003), *In- vs Out-of-Home Drinking*. November 2003 (Download: http://academic/mintel.com).

Mintel (2004), *Attitudes Towards Drinking*. March 2004 (Download: http://academic/mintel.com).

Mintel (2005), *Wine – UK* (Download: http://academic/mintel.com).

Mintel (2007), *British Lifestyles* (Download: http://academic/mintel.com).

Mitchell, D. (1997), 'The Annihilation of Space by the Law: The Roots and Implications of Anti-homeless Laws in the United States', *Antipode* 29: 303–335.

Modood, T. (1992), 'British Muslims and the Rushdie affair', in Donald, J. and Rattansi, A. (eds), *Race', Culture and Difference* (London: Sage), pp. 260–277.

Modood, T. and Berthoud, R. (1997), *Ethnic Minorities in Britain* (London: Policy Studies Institute).

Monkkonen, E.H. (1981), 'A Disorderly People? Urban Order in the Nineteenth and Twentieth Centuries', *The Journal of American History* 68/3: 539–559.

Morean, B. (2005), 'Drinking Country: Sites and Practices in the Production and Expression of Identity', in Wilson, T.M. (ed.), *Drinking Cultures: Alcohol and Identity* (Oxford: Berg), pp. 25–42.

Nairn, K., Higgens, J., Thompson B., Anderson, M. and Fu, N. (2006), "It's Just Like the Teenage Stereotype', You Go Out and Drink and Stuff": Hearing from Young People Who Don't Drink', *Journal of Youth Studies* 9: 287–304.

Nayak, A. (2003), 'Last of the 'Real Geordies'? White Masculinities and the Subcultural Response to Deindustrialisation', *Environment and Planning D: Society and Space* 21: 7–25.

Neff, J.A. and Husaini, B.A. (1985), 'Stress-buffer Properties of Alcohol Consumption: The Role of Urbanicity and Religious Identification', *Journal of Health and Social Behaviour* 26/3: 207–222.

Ní Laoire, C. (2001), 'A Matter of Life and Death?: Men, Masculinities and Staying 'Behind' in Rural Ireland', *Sociologia Ruralis* 41/2: 220–236

Norcliffe, D. (1999), *Islam* (Brighton: Sussex Academic).

Norstrom, T. (1998), 'Effects on Criminal Violence of Different Beverage Types and Private and Public Drinking', *Addiction* 93/5: 689–699.

North West Public Health Observatory (2006), *Local Alcohol Profiles for England.*

Office for National Statistics (2001), *Census 2001* (Available at: http://www.statistics.gov.uk/)

O'Mally, P. and Valverde, M. (2004), 'Pleasure, Freedom and Drugs: The Use of 'Pleasure' in Liberal Governance of Drugs and Alcohol Consumption', *Sociology* 38/1: 25–42.

Orford, J., Johnson, M. and Purser, B. (2004), 'Drinking in Second Generation Black and Asian Communities in the English Midlands', *Addiction Research and Theory* 12/1: 11–30.

Palmer, C. and Thompson, K. (2007), 'The Paradoxes of Football Spectatorship: On-field and Online Expressions of Social Capital Among the "Grog squad". *Sociology of Sport Journal* 24/2: 187–205.

Papagaroufali, E. (1992), 'Uses of Alcohol Amongst Women: Games of Resistance, Power and Pleasure', in Gefou-Madianou, D. (1992), *Alcohol, Gender and Culture* (London: Routledge), pp. 48–70.

Parker, H., William, L. and Aldridge, J. (1998), 'The Normalisation of 'Sensible' Recreational Drug Use: Further Evidence from North-west England Longitudinal Study', *Sociology* 36: 941–964.

Patel, K. (1993), 'Ethnic Minority Access to Services', in Harrison, L (ed.), *Race, Culture and Substance Problems* (Hull: University of Hull), pp. 24–39.

Patterson C.R., Bennett, J.B. and Wiitala, W.L. (2005), 'Healthy and Unhealthy Stress Unwinding: Promoting Health in Small Businesses', *Journal of Business and Psychology* 20: 221–247.

Peace, A. (1992), '"No Fishing without Drinking": The Construction of Social Identity in Rural Ireland', in Gefou-Madianou, D. (1992), *Alcohol, Gender and Culture* (London: Routledge), pp. 167–180.

Pettigrew, S. (2002), 'Consuming Alcohol; Consuming Symbolic Meaning', in Miles, S., Anderson, A. and Meethan, K. (eds), *The Changing Consumer: Markets and Meanings* (Routledge: London), pp. 104–116.

Phillips, D. (2006), 'Parallel Lives? Challenging Discourses of British Muslim Self-Segregation', *Transactions of the Institute of British Geographers* 24: 25–40.

Philo, C. (1992), 'Neglected Rural Geographies: A Review', *Journal of Rural Studies* 8: 193–207.

Philo, C., Parr, H. and Burns, N. (2002), *Alcohol and Mental Health* (draft), published by the Department of Geography and Topographical Science, University of Glasgow at: http://www.geog.gla.ac.uk/olpapers/cphilo015.pdf

Pilcher, J. (1995), *Age and Generations in Modern Britain* (Oxford: Oxford University Press).

Pitkanen, T., Lyyra, A.L. and Pulkkinen, L.(2004), 'Age of Onset of Drinking and the Use of Alcohol in Adulthood: A Follow up Study from Age 8–42 for Females and Males', *Addiction* 100: 652–661.

Plant, M. (1997), *Women and Alcohol: Contemporary and Historical Perspectives* (London: Free Association Books).

Plant, M. and Miller M. (2007), 'Being Taught to Drink: UK Teenagers' Experience', in Järvinen, M. and Room, R. (eds), *Youth Drinking Cultures: European Experiences* (Aldershot: Ashgate), pp. 131–144.

Plant, M. and Plant, M. (1992), *Risk Takers: Alcohol, Drugs, Sex and Youth* (London: Routledge).

Plant, M., Plant, M. (2006), *Binge Britain: Alcohol and the National Response* (Oxford university Press: Oxford)

Plant, M., Single, E. and Stockwell, T. (eds) (2001), *Alcohol: Minimizing the Harm* (London: Free Association Books).

Purvis, M. (1998), 'Popular Institutions', in Langton, J. and Morris, R.J. (eds), *Atlas of Industrial Britain 1780–1914* (London: Methuen).

Putnam, R.D. (2000), *Bowling Alone: The Collapse and Revival of American Community* (New York: Simon and Schuster).

Raco, M. (2003), 'Remaking Place and Securitising Space: Urban Regeneration and the Strategies, Tactics and Practices of Policing in the UK', *Urban Studies* 40/9: 1869–1887.

Radley, A. (1995), 'The Elusory Body and Social Constructionist Theory', *Body and Society* 1: 3–23.

Ramsey, M. (1990), 'Lagerland Lost? An Experiment in Keeping Drinkers Off the Streets in Central Coventry and Elsewhere', *Crime prevention Unit*: Paper 22 (London: Home Office).

Raskin-White, H., Bates, M.E. and Johnson V. (1991), 'Learning to Drink: Familial, Peer and Media Influences', in Pittman, D. and Raskin-White, H. (eds), *Society, Culture and Drinking Patterns Re-Examined* (New Brunswick, NJ: Rutgers Centre for Alcohol Studies).

Richardson, A. and Budd, T. (2003), *Alcohol, Crime and Disorder: a Study of Young Adults* (Home Office: London).

Rickards, L., Fox, K., Roberts, C., Fletcher, L. and Goddard, E. (2004), *Living in Britain: No. 31, Results from the 2002 General Household Survey* (London: TSO).

Roberts, B. (2004), 'Drinking Like a Man: The Paradox of Excessive Drinking for Seventeenth-century Dutch Youths', *Journal of Family History* 29/3: 237–252.

Roberts, M., Turner, C., Osborn, G. and Greenfield, S. (2006), 'A Continental Ambience? Lessons in Managing Alcohol-related Evening and Night-time Entertainment from Four European Capitals', *Urban Studies* 43/7: 1105–1125.

Rojek, C. (1995), *Decentering Leisure. Rethinking Leisure Theory* (London: Sage).

Rose, N. (1999), *Powers to Freedom: Reshaping Political Thought* (Cambridge: Polity Press).

Savage, M. and Warde, A. (1993), *Sociology, Capitalism and Modernity* (New York: Continuum).

Schivelbusch, W. (1992), *Tastes of Paradise* (London: Pantenen).

Scott, A.J. (2000), *The Cultural Economy of Cities: Essays on the Geographies of Image Producing Industries* (London: Sage).

Seeman, M., Seeman, A.Z. and Burdos, A. (1988), 'Powerlessness, Work and Community: A Longtitudinal Study of Alienation and Alcohol Use', *Journal of Health and Social Behaviour* 29/3: 185–198.

Sennett, R. (1977), *The Fall of Public Man* (Cambridge: Cambridge University Press).

Shaikh, Z. and Nax, F. (2000), *A Cultural Cocktail: Asian Women and Alcohol Misuse* (Warks: Aldgate Press).

Share, P. (2003), *A Genuine "Third Place"? Towards an Understanding of the Pub in Contemporary Irish Society*, Paper Presented at the 30th SAI Annual Conference, Cavan, 26 April.

Short, J. (1991), *Imagined Country: Society, Culture and Environment* (London: Routledge).

Shucksmith, J., Glendinning, A. and Hendry, L. (1997), 'Adolescent Drinking Behaviour and the Role of Family life: A Scottish Perspective', *Journal of Adolescence* 20: 85–101.

Skelton, T. and Valentine, G. (1998), *Cool Places: Geographies of Youth Culture* (London: Routledge).

Smart, R.G. and Ogborne, A. (2000), 'Drinking and Heavy Drinking by Students in 18 countries', *Drug and Alcohol Dependence* 60: 315–318.

Smith, L. and Foxcroft, D. (2009), *Drinking in the UK: an Exploration of Trends* (York: Joseph Rowntree Foundation).

Smith, M.A. (1983), 'Social Usage of the Public Drinking House: Changing Aspects of Class and Leisure', *The British Journal of Sociology* 34/3: 367–385.

Smith, N. (1996), *The New Urban Frontier: Gentrification and the Revanchist City* (London: Routledge).

Smith, R. and Womack, S. (2007), *Middle-class are Biggest Abusers of Alcohol.* Telegraph.co.uk 20.10.2007 (http://www.telegraph.co.uk/news/main.jhtml?xml=/news/2007/10/16/ndrinkers116.xml) accessed 22 November.

Social Issues Research Centre (1998), *Social and Cultural Aspects of Drinking: A Report to the Amsterdam Group* (Oxford: The Social Issues Research Centre).

Stallybrass, P. and White, A. (1986), *The Politics and Poetics of Transgression* (London: Methuen).

Stivers, R. (2000), *Hair of the Dog: Irish Drinking and its American Stereotype* (New York: Continuum).

Talbot, D. (2007), *Regulating the Night: Race, Culture and Exclusion in the Making of the Night-time Economy* (Aldershot: Ashgate).

Tatlow, J.R., Clapp, J.D. and Hohman, M.M. (2000), 'The Relationship Between the Geographic Density of Alcohol Outlets and Alcohol-related Hospital Admissions in San Diego County', *Journal of Community Health* 25/1: 79–88.

Teo, P. (1999), 'Singapore's Widows and Widowers Back to the Heart of the Family', in Kenworthy-Teather, E. (ed.), *Embodied Geographies: Spaces, Bodies and Rites of Passage* (London: Routledge), pp. 224–239.

Thomas, C.J. and Bromley, R.D.F. (2000), 'City-centre Revitalization: Problems of Fragmentation and Fear in the Evening and Night-time City', *Urban Studies* 37/8: 1403–1429.

Thomas, M. (2002), 'Out of Control: Emergent Cultural Landscapes and Political Change in Urban Vietnam', *Urban Studies* 39/9: 1611–1624.

Thompson, E.P. (1967), 'Time, Work Discipline and Industrial Capitalism', *Past and Present* 38: 56–97.

Thrift, N. (2004), 'Intensities of Feeling: Towards a Spatial Politics of Affect', *Geografiska Annaler Series B Human Geography* 86 B/1: 57–78.

Tlusty, B.A. (2004), 'Drinking, Family Relations, and Authority in Early Modern Germany', *Journal of Family History* 29/3: 253–273.

Tolia-Kelly, D.P. (2004), 'Materializing Post-colonial Geographies: Examining the Textural Landscapes of Migration in the South Asian Home', *Geoforum* 35: 675–688.

Tolvaven, E. and Jylhä, M.A. (2005), 'Alcohol in Life Story Interviews with Finnish People Aged 90 or Over: Stories of Gendered Morality', *Journal of Aging Studies* 19/4: 419–435.

Treno, A.J., Alaniz, M.L. and Gruenwald, P.J. (2000), 'The Use of Drinking Places by Gender, Age and Ethnic Group: An Analysis of Routine Drinking Activities', *Addiction* 95/4: 537–551.

Tucker, F. and Matthews, H. (2001), 'They Don't Like Girls Hanging Around There: Conflicts Over Recreational Space in Rural Northamptonshire', *Area* 33: 161–168.

Turning Point (2004), *Alcohol Consultation with Young People in England, 2004* (London: Turning Point).

Twigg, L. and Jones, K. (2000), 'Predicting Small-area Health-related Behaviour: A Comparison of Smoking and Drinking indicators', *Social Science and Medicine* 80/11: 9–20.

Unwin, T. (1991), *Wine and the Vine: An Historical Geography of Viticulture and the Wine Trade* (London: Routledge).

Vaillant, G.E. (1983), *The Natural History of Alcoholism* (Cambridge, MA: Harvard University Press).

Valentine, G. (1996), 'Children Should Be Seen and Not Heard? The Role of Children in Public Space', *Urban Geography* 17: 205–220.

Valentine, G. (1998), 'Food and the Production of the Civilised Street', in Fyfe, N. (ed.), *Images of the Street: Planning, Identity and Control of Public Space* (London: Routledge), pp. 192–204.

Valentine, G. (2008), 'Living with Difference: Reflections on Geographies of Encounter', *Progress in Human Geography* 32: 321–335.

Valentine G. and Sporton, D. (2009), 'How Other People See You, It's Like Nothing That's Inside': The Impact of Processes of Dis-identification and Disavowal on Young People's Subjectivities', *Sociology* 1/3: 13–37.

Valentine, G., Holloway, S.L. and Bingham, N. (2002), 'The Digital Generation? Children, ICT and the Everyday Nature of Social Exclusion', *Antipode* 34: 296–315.

Valentine, G., Holloway, S.L. and Jayne, M. (2007a), 'Drinking Places: Young People and Cultures of Alcohol Consumption in Rural Environments', *Journal of Rural Studies* 24: 28–40.

Valentine, G., Holloway, S.L., Jayne, M. and Knell, C. (2007b), *Drinking Places: Where People Drink and Why* (York: Joseph Rowntree Foundation).

Valentine, G., Holloway, S.L. and Jayne, M. (2010), 'Generational Patterns of Alcohol Consumption: Continuity and Change', *Health and Place* 16/5: 916–925.

Valentine, G., Jayne M. and Holloway, S.L. (2010), 'Contemporary Cultures of Abstinence and the Night-time Economy: Muslim Attitudes Towards Alcohol and the Implications for Social Cohesion', *Environment and Planning A* 42/1: 8–22.

Valentine, G., Sporton, D. and Bang-Nielsen K. (2009), 'Identities and Belonging: A Study of Somali Refugee and Asylum Seekers Living in the UK and Denmark', *Environment and Planning D: Society and Space* 2/4: 23–37.

Valverde, M. (2003), 'Police Science, British Style: Pub Licensing and Knowledges of Urban Disorder', *Economy and Society* 32/2: 234–252.

van Zundert, R.M.P., van der Horst, H.L., Vermulst, A. and Engels, R. (2006), 'Pathways to Alcohol Use among Dutch Students in Regular Education and Education for Adolescents with Behavioral Problems: The Role of Parental Alcohol Use, General Parenting Practices and Alcohol-specific Parenting Practices', *Journal of Family Psychology* 20: 456–457.

Vertovec, S. (1998), 'Young Muslims in Keighley, West Yorkshire: Cultural Identity, Context and Community', in Vertovec, S. and Rogers, A. (eds), *Muslim European Youth: Reproducing Ethnicity, Religion and Culture* (Aldershot: Ashgate), pp. 87–101.

Vertovec, S. (ed.) (2001), *South Asians Overseas* (Cambridge: Cambridge University Press).

Visser, M. (1991), *The Rituals of Dinner: The Origins, Evolution, Eccentricities and Meaning of Table Manners* (New York: Grove Weidenfeld).

Vives, R., Nebot, M., Ballestin, M., Diez, E. and Villalbi, J.R. (2000), 'Changes in Alcohol Consumption Patterns Among Schoolchildren in Barcelona', *European Journal of Epidemiology* 16: 27–32.

Walsh, K. (2006), 'British Expatriate Belongings: Mobile Homes and Transnational Homing', *Home Cultures* 3: 123–144.

Ward, C. (1990), *The Child in the Country* (London: Bedford Square Press).

Waterson, J. (2000), *Women and Alcohol in Social Context: Mothers Ruin Revisited* (London: Palgrave).

The Way we Were – Millennium Special Edition (1999), The Sentinel Supplement, p. 10.

Wickrama, K., Conger, R., Wallace, L. and Elder, G. (1999), 'The Intergenerational Transmission of Health-risk Behaviours: Adolescent Lifestyles and Gender Moderating Effects', *Journal of Health and Behaviour* 40: 258–272.

Wilson, T.M. (ed.) (2005), *Drinking Cultures* (Oxford: Berg).

Winchester, H.P.M., McGuirk, P.M. and Everett, K. (1999), 'Schoolies Week as a Rite of Passage: A Study of Celebration and Control', in Kenworthy-Teather, E. (ed.), *Embodied Geographies: Spaces, Bodies and Rites of Passage* (London: Routledge), pp. 59–77

Winlow, S. and Hall, S. (2006), *Violent Night: Urban Leisure and Contemporary Culture* (Oxford: Berg).

Wittman, F.D. (1997), 'Local Control to Prevent Problems of Alcohol Availability; Experience in Californian Communities', in Plant, M., Single, E. and Stockwell,

T. (eds), *Alcohol: Minimizing the Harm* (London: Free Association Books), pp. 43–71.

Wolcott, H.F. (1974), *African Beer Gardens of Bulawayo: Integrated Drinking in a Segregated Society* (New Brunswick, NJ: Rutgers Center of Alcohol Studies).

Wood, N. (2002), '"Once More with Feeling": Putting Emotion into Geographies of Music', in Bondi, L., et al. (eds), *Subjectivities, Knowledges and Feminist Geographies: The Subjects and Ethics of Social Research* (Lanham, MD: Rowman and Littlefield), pp. 57–72.

World Health Organization (2000), *International Guide for Monitoring Alcohol Consumption and Related Alcohol Harm* (Stockholm: World Health Organization).

World Health Organization (2001), *Alcohol in the European Region: Consumption, Harm and Policies* (Stockholm: World Health Organization).

World Health Organization (2004), *Global Status Report: Alcohol Policy* (Stockholm: World Health Organization).

Wright, L. (1999), *Young People and Alcohol* (London: Health Education Authority).

Wyness, M. (1997), 'Parental Responsibilities, Social Policy and the Maintenance of Boundaries', *Sociological Review* 45/2: 304–324.

Wynne, D. and O'Connor, J. (1998), 'Consumption and the Postmodern City', *Urban Studies* 35: 841–64.

Yarwood, R. (2001), 'Crime and Policing in the British Countryside: Some Agendas for Contemporary Geographical Research', *Sociologia Ruralis* 41/2: 201–219 Blackwell.

Yarwood, R. (2005), 'Crime Concern and Policing in the Countryside: Evidence from Parish Councillors in West Mercia Constabulary, England', *Policing and Society* 15/1: 63–82

Yip, A. (2004), 'Negotiating Space with Family and Kin in Identity Construction: The Narratives of British Non-heterosexual Muslims', *The Sociological Review* 2: 336–350.

York, J.L., Welte, J., Hirsch, J., Hoffman, J.H. and Barnes G. (2004), 'Association of Age of First Drink with Current Alcohol Drinking Variables in a National General Population Sample', *Alcoholism: Clinical and Experimental Research* 28: 1379–1387.

Young, K. (2002), 'The Memory of the Flesh: The Family Body in Somatic Psychology', *Body and Society* 8/3: 25–47.

Yu, J. (1998), 'Perceived Parents/peer Attitudes and Alcohol-related Behaviours: An Analysis of the Impact of the Drinking Age Law', *Substance Use and Misuse* 33: 2687–2702.

Yu, J. (2003), 'The Association Between Parental Alcohol-related Behaviours and Children's Drinking', *Drug and Alcohol Dependence* 69: 253–262.

Yu, J., Varone, R. and Shacket, R.W. (1997), '*A Fifteen-Year Review of Drinking Age Laws: Preliminary Findings of the 1996 New York State Youth Alcohol*

Survey (Albany, NY: New York State Office of Alcoholism and Substance Abuse Services).

Zokaei, S. and Phillips, D. (2000), 'Altruism and Intergenerational Relations among Muslims in Britain', *Current Sociology* 48: 45–58.

Zukin, S. (1995), *The Cultures of Cities* (Oxford: Blackwell).

Zukin, S. (1998), 'Urban Lifestyles: Diversity and Standardization in Spaces of Consumption', *Urban Studies* 35: 825–839.

Index